"**Breathing Space** offers insightful observations about how the overglut can quickly overwhelm us. I thought I had done a good job of limiting my subscriptions, until I realized I still wasn't even reviewing 25% of them, for the very reasons Jeff said. They may be worth the money, but they're not worth my time!"

James G. Kidd, Walt Disney, Design & Engineering

"Many people spend half their time simply 'getting organized' without a clear plan, so that any attempt at efficiency becomes an exercise in wheel-spinning. **Breathing Space** shows you how to change your attitude, a fundamental component in regaining control over the rat race."

Janice Johnson, columnist, Knight Ridder Newspapers

"Some have likened our information glut to attempting to sip water through a straw from a fire hydrant. Jeff Davidson helps readers create the calm waters where they can focus their time. **Breathing Space** makes a difference on and off the job."

Terry L. Paulson, Ph.D., author, *They Shoot Managers Don't They?* and *Secrets Every Teen Needs to Know*

"This book taught me a lot. The most important thing— and I needed this badly—is your concept that 'keeping up' is illusory. On behalf of my wife, as well as myself, thank you for valuable insights."

Alan Cimberg, veteran sales trainer

"This book will help all people who work in our fast-paced society. Jeff Davidson clearly explains how to achieve breathing space in a world where stress-induced diseases are increasing due to time-pressure."

Donald Huffmire, Ph.D., Professor of Business Administration, University of Connecticut

"Anyone as accomplished as Jeff Davidson certainly has a lot to teach about taking control of our lives and in **Breathing Space** he wastes no time in getting right to the critical issues."

Russell Wild, Editor, *Prevention Magazine* health books and author, *Boost Your Brain Power*

"In the age of the technology explosion, the media blitz-krieg and the information deluge, we all feel pressured to accomplish more, buy more, and know more in less time. **Breathing Space** challenges us to stop and assess our needs and priorities; to take a rational approach to living."

Judith Pearson, Ph.D., Licensed Professional Counselor, Trainer and Consultant

"Jeff Davidson drives the field of inspirational/how-to authors, and lives by his words."

Clifford D. McGoon, Vice President, International Association of Business Communicators

"I've read several of Jeff Davidson's books and enjoyed them all. **Breathing Space** is timely, on target, and reassuring, and focused exactly where I'm heading."

Karla, President, Karla's Great Cheesecakes

"Each month, our editors review *hundreds* of business/career books and articles. Jeff Davidson's advice and insights are consistently among the most practical, useful and timely we encounter."

Ray Marsili, Publisher, *Sales & Marketing Digest*

"**Breathing Space** offers the harried executive of the 90's a practical way to control the flood of paper and information that threatens productivity and peace of mind."

Shirley L. Rooker, President, Call for Action, Inc.

"The theme and concepts expressed in **Breathing Space** are powerful; those of us on the unending, hyper-treadmill of life in the 1990's have been waiting for this book."

"Once again Jeff Davidson has captured a profound concept and simplified it for ease of reading and immediate application. **Breathing Space** has a significant message for those who want to reduce clutter, create space to grow and enjoy the moment more fully."

"Jeff Davidson is a one-man, on-going energy machine and anyone can learn a great deal by reading **Breathing Space**."

"**Breathing Space** underscores a concept crucial to emotional health and satisfying relationships—keeping one's worklife gratifying and contained."

"**Breathing Space** is a resourceful guide for readers ranging from alcoholics to dropouts, and anyone else who seeks to regain control of his life. It offers help to those 'out of step,' enabling them to acquire a comfortable cadence."

"**Breathing Space** is must reading if you wish to survive in the 90's."

"Jeff Davidson's 10 commandments of sound deskmanship inspired me—for the first time in my life—to clear my desk top. What a wonderful gift to myself!"

Barry A. Sultanoff, M.D., physician, Bethesda Health Associates

"Jeff Davidson has done it again—he has pinpointed a problem that affects all of us, and attacked it head on, with wisdom and keen insight. I like his problem-solving approach and his down-to-earth style."

Jefferson D. Bates, author, *Writing with Precision* and *Dictating Effectively*

"As we careen toward the year 2000, I'm glad Jeff Davidson is there to remind us how to balance our personal and professional lives."

Barbara Feiner, Executive Editor, Creative Age Publications

"**Breathing Space** will help executives, entrepreneurs and busy people in all occupations achieve, earn and enjoy themselves more. The advice on getting rid of clutter, in particular, is simple, direct and dynamically effective."

Bob Sweeney, Managing Director, Olympic Figure & Fitness Clubs, Halifax, England

"Life is priorities. Jeff Davidson has captured the essence of clarifying life's complexities in this powerful, vital book."

Bill Brooks, author, *Niche Selling: How to Find Your Customer in a Crowded Market*

"Take some time from your busy schedule to read **Breathing Space**. The principles introduced will repay you many times over in time and space gained."

Linda Stern, Contributing Editor, *Home Office Computing*

"After reading **Breathing Space** I'm more motivated than ever to deal with the pace of the 90's and the 21st century."

Dr. Richard S. Katz, Doctor of Optometry

"Take this book's approach and you'll literally create some breathing space in your life; this approach not only makes sense, it takes the self-manipulation tactics out of managing your day by putting you in real control. You'll not only feel better, you'll be more productive in the areas of your life where you want to be productive."

Sally M. Scanlon, Managing Editor, National Institute of Business Management

"I'll do better than endorse it—I'll buy it."

Craig Stolz, former editor, *Washington Dossier*

"**Breathing Space** makes compelling issues easy to understand and digest."

Sanford W. Kahn, President, Center for Economic Development

"This book teaches you to pro-actively guard your time and space. It's a riveting eye-opener."

Lynn L. Lucchetti, Colonel, U.S. Air Force Reserves

"An overcrowded schedule stifles innovation and creativity, which are both essential elements in humankind's future progress. **Breathing Space** is a great help in getting organized and avoiding the pitfalls posed by the tera-byte information glut."

Dr. N. Paul Kuin, Senior Scientist, NASA, National Space Science Data Center and ST Systems Corporation

"A small volume that is big on answers to the whys of our cluttered existence and how to spring loose from the trap."

Joel Makower, author, *The Green Consumer*

"Very timely and sound advice on living, working and thriving in today's fast-paced, high-pressure society."

Deidre K. Murray, Director, National Council of Career Women

"Following the guidelines in **Breathing Space** is bound to improve anyone's overall sense of well-being."

Joan Rabinor, Ph.D., licensed clinical social worker in private practice

"A remarkable blueprint for living and working in a rapidly changing world. It's easy to see now why time management will no longer work, and why **Breathing Space** is just what the doctor ordered."

Ken Dychtwald, Ph.D., President of Age Wave, and author, *Age Wave: The Challenges and Opportunities of an Aging America*

"Most people who are managing the world are not very good at managing themselves. Get your own life in order first before you begin bossing others.

"A good place to start is with **Breathing Space,** Jeff Davidson's latest and greatest."

Al Ries, Chairman of Trout & Ries, and co-author of *Positioning: The Battle for Your Mind*

"I think **Breathing Space** is Jeff's best book yet. I'm giving a copy to each of my friends."

Mrs. Jeff Davidson

OTHER BOOKS BY

JEFF DAVIDSON

CASH TRAPS: SMALL BUSINESS SECRETS FOR REDUCING COSTS AND IMPROVING CASH FLOW (Wiley, 1992)

65 WAYS TO MAKE YOUR BANK WORK FOR YOU (Consumer Reports Books, 1992)

THE DOMINO EFFECT: HOW TO GROW YOUR BUSINESS THE DOMINO'S PIZZA WAY by Don Vlcek with Jeff Davidson (Business One-Irwin, 1991)

MARKETING TO HOME-BASED BUSINESS (Business One-Irwin, 1991)

YOU CAN START YOUR OWN BUSINESS (Washington Publications, 1991)

POWER AND PROTOCOL FOR GETTING TO THE TOP: THE IMAGE, THE MOVES AND THE SMARTS FOR BUSINESS AND SOCIAL SUCCESS (Shapolsky, 1991)

AVOIDING THE PITFALLS OF STARTING YOUR OWN BUSINESS (Shapolsky, 1991)

BLOW YOUR OWN HORN: HOW TO GET AHEAD AND GET NOTICED (Berkley, 1991)

SELLING TO THE GIANTS: HOW TO BECOME A KEY SUPPLIER TO LARGE CORPORATIONS (Liberty Press division of Tab/McGraw-Hill, 1991)

HOW TO HAVE A GOOD YEAR EVERY YEAR by Dave Yoho & Jeff Davidson (Berkley, 1991)

MARKETING YOUR CONSULTING AND PROFESSIONAL SERVICES (Wiley, 1990)

MARKETING FOR THE HOME-BASED BUSINESS (Bob Adams, Inc., 1990)

THE MARKETING SOURCEBOOK FOR SMALL BUSINESS (Wiley, 1989)

MARKETING ON A SHOESTRING (Wiley, 1988)

GETTING NEW CLIENTS (Wiley, 1987)

HOW TO BE A "TEN" IN BUSINESS, by Don Beveridge and Jeff Davidson (Business One-Irwin, 1987)

MARKETING YOUR COMMUNITY (Public Technology, Inc., 1987)

CHECKLIST MANAGEMENT (National Press, 1986)

BREATHING SPACE

SPACE

LIVING
AND WORKING
AT A COMFORTABLE
PACE IN
A SPED-UP SOCIETY

JEFF DAVIDSON

MasterMedia Limited

NEW YORK

To Robert Fritz for opening the door
to a world of new choices,

and to the next Millennium.

Library of Congress Cataloging-in-Publication Data

Davidson, Jeff.
    Breathing space : living and working at a comfortable pace in
a sped-up society / Jeff Davidson.
        p.   cm.
    Includes bibliographical references.
    ISBN 0-942361-32-6
    1. Time management—United States.   I. Title.
HN90.T5D38   1991
640'.43—dc20   91-60811
                                                       CIP

Printed in the U.S.A.

Manufactured through Martin Cook Associates, Ltd.

10   9   8   7   6   5   4   3   2   1

CONTENTS

PART
I

THE ROOT CAUSES OF THE PRESSURE YOU FEEL

PART
II

HAND TOOLS

PART
III

POWER TOOLS

PART
IV

CEREBRAL TOOLS

PART
V

METAPHYSICAL TOOLS

ACKNOWLEDGMENTS

Many people contributed to **Breathing Space**. Nancy Davidson, Ph.D., made extensive, keen insights that helped guide me every step of the way. Jill Korroch made incisive observations. Juliet Bruce and Ed Wong offered key copy edits. Richard Connor convinced me to initiate the project. Judith Briles and Edie Fraser led me to MasterMedia. Kate McKeown, Holland Cooke, and Marilyn Liebrenz-Himes, Ph.D., offered detailed reviews and criticism. Martin Horn, Alan Schlaifer, and Robert Bookman provided in-depth commentary. Colleen Blessing, Norman Lerner, Ph.D., Emanuel Davidson, Richard Davidson, Shirley Davidson, Susan Davidson, Sally Ulrich, Chuck Dean, and Peter Hicks all provided valuable input.

I wish to thank Alvin Toffler, William Broad, Neil Postman, Ph.D., Dennis Hensley, Barbara Hemphill, Marshall McLuhan, Ph.D., Alan Watts, Pat Mc-Callum, Stanley M. Davis, Ph.D., John Kenneth Galbraith, Ph.D., and Robert Fritz for their subject matter expertise. I would like to thank Bob Antler for designing the cover, Lois Lapid for fine catalog copy, Jim Baumann for his editorial, publishing, and marketing expertise, Martin Cook, Alex Hoyt,

Rita Marcus, Karen Romer, Clare Pini, and Tony Colao for the excellence they embody, and, most of all, Susan S. Stautberg for her vision, leadership, and support.

FOREWORD

In deciding to write this book, Jeff Davidson told me that he had one major concern:

> "Given society's rapid pace, with most people frequently under pressure to get things done, would enough people believe it is possible to gain breathing space and to work and live at a comfortable pace?"

In the seven years I've known Jeff, I've been amazed at the frequency and duration of the breathing space he finds for himself and his family—despite the fact that he is one of the most accomplished people I've met. Jeff has an uncanny ability to help others also find breathing space. Through his professional speaking engagements, he has helped countless numbers of people take small steps that generate large rewards.

Having personally benefited from Jeff's counsel, I can say unconditionally that what you are about to read will change your life for the better.

With Jeff's approach, you feel good about making changes—you experience no internal wars, no reluctance. What he has to say is on target; you find yourself eager to act on his suggestions.

Jeff has structured this book so that the average page can be read comfortably in about a minute. I know you'll find, as I have, that **Breathing Space** is a most useful, enjoyable book. The information and advice contained in this classic has irrevocably changed my life for the better and can do the same for you.

Bill Thompson,
Producer/Host,
"Between the Lines,"
Associated Press National Radio Network

INTRODUCTION

When you have eliminated the impossible, whatever remains, however im-
probable, must be the truth.
—SHERLOCK HOLMES, *SIGN OF FOUR*
BY SIR ARTHUR CONAN DOYLE

"If I could only get a little breathing space." How often has that thought come up for you lately? Probably all too frequently. Meanwhile,

❏ Your desk is piled high with papers;
❏ You continually find yourself racing with the clock;
❏ You are deluged with projects and tasks right now.

If so, *you are far from being alone.* The challenges you face are linked to challenges faced by our entire culture.

Unquestionably, the pace of society has sped up. New buildings are erected in a month. Wars can be fought and won in weeks, not months or years.

1

Books can be written and published in less than ten days. Movies are deemed smash hits or duds following their first weekend's box office receipts. Prescription glasses are ready in one hour. Gourmet meals can be delivered to your door in minutes. Fax machines transmit pages in seconds.

Conversely, commuting takes longer. So does shopping. Learning new programs, instructions, or ways to increase productivity takes its toll. Juggling work and domestic responsibilities is a growing challenge. Among working adults, whom do you know today who consistently has an unfilled schedule?

Beyond the pressures you face, what you may not have realized is that nearly everyone is feeling the same way; we appear to be a society of people in a hurry. Is *frantic* any way to exist as a people? Is it any way to run your life?

Reporting Live from Main Street

- ❑ The Louis Harris Organization found that "since 1973 the number of hours worked by Americans increased by 20 percent, from 40.6 to 48.8 per week, while the amount of leisure available to the average person has dropped by 32 percent."

- ❑ A front-page *New York Times* story entitled "Most People Feel They Never Have Any Time" discussed the widespread feeling that "there is too much to do."

❑ A *Prevention Magazine* survey on health found that 40 percent of our adult population—71 million people—"suffer from stress every day of their lives and find they can sleep no more than six hours a night."

❑ In a *Time* magazine cover story entitled "Drowsy America," the director of Stanford University's sleep center concluded that "most Americans no longer know what it feels like to be fully alert."

Why are so many individuals today overwhelmed, deluged, and exhausted? My eleven-year inquiry reveals that powerful social and cultural forces indiscriminately are turning each of us into human whirlwinds charging about to get things done in "fast forward." This is not how it has to be.

The critical capability of the 1990's is controlling your life despite scores of tasks and activities competing for your attention. Finding a little breathing space seemingly is more difficult with each passing day. Nevertheless, you still wish to gain or regain control of your life, and to feel good about the process. My goal is to help you create a more favorable future for yourself.

As an author and speaker, I have a vision. I see our society composed of people leading balanced lives with rewarding careers, happy home lives, and the ability to enjoy themselves.

I wrote **Breathing Space: Living and Working at a Comfortable Pace in a Sped-Up Society** to provide you and other busy people a way out of this dilemma without requiring radical changes in how you live or what you do; to introduce sensible, implementable solutions and fresh perspectives that you will know and feel are right for you.

Time Management Is a Dated Concept

The conditions surrounding us have changed radically, even since the late 1980s. The basic approach that many people take to solve their tense predicament is to bone up on time management techniques. There is no practical value, however, in becoming more adept in dealing with the world the way it used to be.

If it seems as though the harder you strive to keep up, the farther behind you get, it could be that you're on the wrong track, against the wrong foe.

A few days after attending a time management seminar, or a few hours after reading time management books or articles, you can quickly become convinced that maintaining personal control is futile. Though such programs are well meaning, offering solutions without understanding the problem is like putting a Band-Aid on an eight-inch gash.

It's okay to apply personal control techniques, once you fully understand the larger forces at play. Otherwise, gaining more hours or days is of little value. Without having a wide-screen perspective as to what is contributing to the pressures you feel, whether your days are twenty-four hours or thirty-six hours long, you're likely to use them up in much the same way as you do now. You'll be *looking for breathing space* in all the wrong places. And, once again, you'll arrive at the conclusion that you have none.

No, my fellow voyager, longer days or weeks, if you could have them, are not the answer to the relief you seek. "Everything would be okay if only I had more time" is a delusion that ill serves you. ⏎

Your real quest is to fully engage in life with what you have, smack dab in the midst of the ever-changing dynamics of our existence. It is rooted in gaining whatever fulfillment means to you, *within twenty-four days, and seven-day weeks,* and however many more years you have on earth. It is realizing that your perceptions—as much as your actions—dictate the amount and quality of breathing space you enjoy.

Time is not your enemy. It is the most loyal ally on which you can depend. Though it often seems to speed up or slow down, for all practical purposes, it is as constant a factor as can exist in your life.

The Path to Breathing Space

In this society, in this era, extreme obstacles potentially thwart your search for contentment. You can, however, gain a stronger sense of control and live at a more comfortable pace.

First, we'll confirm many of your suspicions, and focus on why *merely being alive* today and participating as a functioning member of society guarantees that your day, week, month, year, and life, and your physical, emotional, and spiritual energy, will be depleted easily without the proper vantage point from which to approach each day and conduct your life.

As we proceed, you may find chapters 2 through 7, the first third of the book, to be startling, even upsetting. This part won't take long to get through, but its effect on you may be profound.

> If you're serious about improving the quality of the rest of your life and committed to regularly attaining breathing space, the dead-last thing you need is another quick-fix approach to happiness.

Just as the allies' stunning victory in the Persian Gulf was achieved through intensive study of the adversary—his resources, communication and supply lines, strategies, battle maneuvers, strengths, weaknesses, underlying motivations, inconsistencies, and contingencies—your stunning ascension to a greater sense of breathing space will result from intensive examination of what is obstructing you.

On the path to breathing space, we'll begin with a compelling, in-your-face portrait of our frenzied existence. This includes a discussion of five "mega-realities" ("mega-trends" already in effect) that can easily diminish your sense of breathing space.

The startling reality will be more than offset by principles and perspectives that can be absorbed, adopted, and used, now. You'll find that you can acquire the space you want and need in your life.

Respecting the pressures you currently face, I've kept **Breathing Space** to 209 uncrowded pages, divided into twenty-two concise chapters. I seek to deftly aid you in your quest to live and work at a comfortable pace.

We'll cover how to:

❑ Attain breathing space when apparently none is available;
❑ Use completions to stop racing the clock;
❑ Deal with other people's clutter.

We'll also explore the steps to conditioning your immediate environment to support you more fully. We'll conclude with a new set of tools—tools of the mind—to help you master having breathing space.

I hope you read and reread these pages on your quest to achieve a new level of personal control and self-determination. Please share any breakthroughs you experience with others, because, after all, everyone needs breathing space.

PART

I

THE ROOT CAUSES
OF THE PRESSURE
YOU FEEL

Who Sped Up the Clock?

Time is
  Too slow for those who Wait,
  Too swift for those who Fear,
  Too long for those who Grieve,
  Too short for those who Rejoice,
But for those who Love
  Time is not.
                    —HENRY VAN DYKE, SCULPTOR
                    AND ARTIST

Remember how slowly the days passed when you were a child? An eighty-mile car trip seemed endless. It took forever for summer to come. When it finally did, by late-July, summer seemed interminable.

Have you ever wondered why everything apparently passes so slowly to youngsters? Basic arithmetic reveals that for a two-year-old, the next year will represent 33 percent of her life thus far, whereas for a nineteen-year-old, the next year represents 5

11

percent, and for a thirty-nine-year-old, only 2.5 percent.

More than anything else, however, the young child's *perceptions* influence how she experiences life. A toddler has few markers that delineate the passage of time. On the first of each month, she pays no rent or mortgage. She has no job, and does not commute.

She is likely to be regularly clothed, bathed, and cared for. She arises each day with no agenda, no "to do" list. She does experience hunger, irritation, and sleepiness, and she has some favorite activities—her major activity is play.

Outside information comes to her from her parents or other "tall" sources such as the big, bright, talking box in the living room; or toys—musical, speaking, and otherwise. She learns to anticipate certain activities, such as lunch.

Each day brings new wonders, giggles, whimpers. Meanwhile, she has no report to finish, no checkbook to balance, no cross-town meetings. She does not even wear a watch.

Your life is a bit more complicated—the all-time understatement!—and is related increasingly to how society has become more complex. Independent of who you are or what you do for a living, you are busy—often extremely busy.

If you continually feel pressured, don't take it personally! The same dilemma confronts millions of others; you are part of the most time-pressed population in history. From fast-food counter clerks, to high-powered executives, to retirees, few people today have what they consider to be breathing space—in which to reflect, unwind, truly relax, or simply *be*.

Each moment, you are being bombarded on all sides, although the shelling is invisible. The "intake overglut" wreaks havoc on the receptive capacities of the unwary. Yet you can break away from the pack that idly ingests all the information, noise, and distraction that come its way. Despite the ever-escalating array of obstacles, you can attain breathing space.

REPORTING LIVE FROM THE FRONT

Having long grappled with the perils of a high-pressure existence, I've found that it is essential to understand how we collectively and individually got to our current, hectic state of affairs *before* exploring principles that lead to resolution. You've got to eat your broccoli before you get dessert!

So sit in a comfortable chair, get munchies (if you think you need to), and be prepared to boldly go where you haven't gone before.

Civilization 101—The Short Course

Now then . . . Civilization has witnessed four major ages, including the age of hunting and gathering, the age of agriculture, the age of industry, and the *emerging* information age. I say "emerging" because it hasn't arrived yet. We've only danced around the periphery in a nether land I call the "over-information era." As we'll see in the next few chapters, the over-information era is the major root of the pressure you feel.

Humankind's orientation to time and distance has changed constantly over the ages, but never so much as in the last few decades. With a global communications network in place, as any satellite dish or fax machine user knows, mass and interpersonal communications across continents have become instantaneous.

As a species, we live longer. The life span of the average caveman was nineteen. The life expectancy in Europe in 1392 was thirty-eight. The life span in America in 1892 was forty-nine. Today, it is seventy-two for American men, seventy-seven for women, and quickly rising for both sexes. We're living longer, yet, for many people, most days race by.

The faster we're able to travel or to gain new information, the greater our expectations regarding what can and needs to be accomplished in our lives. We all seek to do more.

A day is still twenty-four hours, but it seems to shrink in the face of more to do or greater expectations about what has to be done. Five factors, or mega-realities if you will, are simultaneously contributing to the *perceptual* erosion of personal time.

The mega-realities include:

❏ Population growth;
❏ An expanding volume of knowledge;
❏ Mass media growth and electronic addiction;
❏ The paper trail culture; and
❏ An overabundance of choices.

Let's see how these factors combine to squelch your sense of breathing space.

2

Population and Your Life

—

Every two years and nine months, the world population grows by the current population of the United States—252 million people.

—

It took from the beginning of creation to 1850 A.D. for human population to reach 1 billion. Human population actually varied little from 500 B.C. to 1750 A.D., remaining below the one-half-billion mark. It grew to 2 billion by 1930, 3 billion by 1960, 4 billion by 1979, and 5 billion by 1987, with 6 billion by 1996, and billions more within a few decades.

The world of your parents' childhood, and of your own childhood, is gone. Forever.

FRESH AIR: The ability to simply acknowledge the world as it is—no modest task—helps you to let go of the erroneous notion that somehow things will return to the "good old days." Regardless of what

16

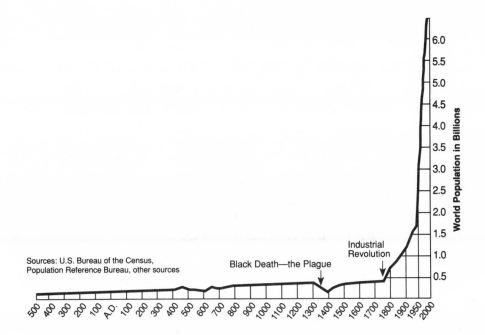

Sources: U.S. Bureau of the Census,
Population Reference Bureau, other sources

Black Death—the Plague

Industrial
Revolution

World Population in Billions

you or I think about it, we are never going back to
how it used to be. The present is *crowded* and becoming more so.

The geometric growth in human population now
permeates and dominates every aspect of the
planet—its resources, the environment, and the life
of each person. Bummer. It also results in more of
each individual's day, including yours and mine,
being consumed in the attempt to maintain quality
of life.

Along with advancing populations, growing international economic competition means that
you're probably working harder now than you did
eight years ago, while not getting paid much more.
Why?

REPORTING LIVE FROM THE WORLD POPULATION
BUREAU IN WASHINGTON

❏ In twenty-four hours, world population (births minus deaths) will increase by another *265,000 people*, as it does each day.

❏ More than half of all the people who *have ever lived* on earth are alive today. The dead are now in the minority.

❏ Within thirty years, Nigeria, Indonesia, Pakistan, and Brazil will have populations roughly equal to the current U.S. population, which will remain fourth in population behind China, India, and the Soviet Union.

❏ World population will reach 10.5 to 11.5 billion before "zero population growth" will occur, if it does at all.

After World War II, the United States was the only industrialized nation with its factories intact. Our superior mass production and distribution facilities yielded twenty-five years of unparalleled prosperity. As education and skill levels advance globally, however, more nations have an effect on, and directly compete with, the economies of one another. For example, last year, 52 percent of engineering Ph.D.'s from American colleges were granted to foreign students.

The success of foreign competition in the United States and in world markets requires a concerted, diligent effort on the part of our domestic corporations and their employees to remain competitive.

U.S. firms hire and retain employees who work harder and longer, and for less. The U.S. Bureau of Labor Statistics reports that between 1981 and 1987, the average annual increase in the productivity of the American manufacturing worker was five times more than the increase in average annual yearly wages.

REPORTING LIVE FROM THE CENSUS BUREAU IN WASHINGTON

- ❏ In 1960, our population was 180 million. It is now 252 million—72 million more in one generation.

- ❏ Our growing population has *not* dispersed over the nation's 5.4 million square miles. About 97 percent of the U.S. population resides on 3 percent of the land mass.

- ❏ Half of our population resides within fifty miles of the Atlantic or the Pacific Ocean.

- ❏ Seventy-five percent of the U.S. population live in urban areas, with 80 percent predicted by the end of the nineties.

Note: Please skip the boxes if numbers overcome or confound you.

Not only do tenacious competitors sell us cars and VCRs, they also cause our CEOs and top managers to lose sleep thinking of new ways to generate greater productivity from an already pressured workforce.

The Population at Home—The Sardine Effect

Independent of foreign economic pressure, our society grows more complex as a function of its own increasing population and lack of dispersion. This complexity also results in more effort simply to maintain standards of living.

More densely packed urban areas have resulted predictably in a gridlock of the nation's transportation systems. Yes, it is taking you longer merely to drive a few blocks; no, it's not your imagination, it's not the day of the week or the season, and it's not going to subside soon. Our population and road use grow faster than our ability to repair highways, bridges, and arteries.

If you drive, hereafter consider it your civic duty to keep your car well tuned.

City planners report there will be no clear solution to gridlock for decades, and all population studies reveal that our nation's metropolitan areas will become home *to an even greater percentage of the population*. Even lower-populated urban areas will face unending traffic dilemmas.

If only the gridlock were confined to commuter arteries. However, shoppers (shoplock), air travelers

REPORTING LIVE FROM THE DEPARTMENT OF
TRANSPORTATION IN WASHINGTON

- ❏ Vehicles (primarily cars) are multiplying twice as fast as people, currently approaching 400 million vehicles, compared with 165 million registered motorists.

- ❏ Eighty-six percent of commuters get to work by automobile. Eighty-four percent of inner city travel is by automobile.

- ❏ The average American commutes 157,600 miles to work during his working life, equal to six times around the earth. Commuting snarls are increasing.

- ❏ Three-quarters of the nation's 575,000 bridges were built before 1938, and nearly half are structurally deficient.

- ❏ One stalled automobile on an overloaded highway can cause 15,000 people to sit and wait in their cars for an hour or more. Yet, one car in four is low on oil by a quart or more; 33 percent have underinflated tires; 50 percent have corroded battery terminals; 50 percent have a dirty air filter.

(flightlock), vacationers (resortlock), even campers—everyone in motion is or will be feeling its effects. American or not, your breathing space is likely to be under siege for years to come.

FRESH AIR: All the ways of beating traffic, getting up earlier and other maneuvers, while they can provide some benefit, eventually yield to the inevitable: If you presently live in and/or commute to an urban area, you can move closer to your job, change your job, or self-employ. Otherwise, gridlock will be a part of your life each day. Your challenge will be to find enjoyment in the midst of it all. Fortunately, it can be done.

Over-informed,
Overwhelmed, and
Under-served

Data, data everywhere, but not
a thought to think.
—SONYA YESPUH, MARKETING
RESEARCHER AND CONSULTANT

Before he was twenty-four, your grandfather acquired enough knowledge to make a good living for
his whole life. "Such a deal" is *not* available to you.
The speed at which new information and data are
developed and disseminated transcends your ability
to keep pace. Worse, what you learned yesterday
may have little or no value today.

As human beings, we seek greater understanding
and breakthroughs in biology, medicine, defense,
and agriculture and so forth. The volume of new
knowledge published in any field is enormous and

easily exceeds anyone's ability to keep pace. Every-one today fears that he or she is underinformed.

❑ In its 140th year, the Smithsonian Institute in Washington, D.C., added 942,000 items to its collections.
❑ Even our language keeps expanding. Since 1966, more than 60,000 words have been added to the English language—equal to half or more of the total words in some languages.

In fact, the actual discharge of information spewing forth since the phrase "information explosion" was first coined dwarfs the original meaning.

WITHIN EIGHT YEARS, HALF OF OUR TECHNICAL KNOWLEDGE WILL HAVE BEEN REPLACED:

Every other page in all the texts on *A*IDS, *b*io-mass, *c*hemical dependency, *d*iet, *e*lectronic funds transfer, *f*ire retardation, *g*ynecology, *h*ydrogen fission, *i*mmunology, *j*et propulsion, *k*inetics, *l*inear motion, *m*eteorology, *n*ovas, *o*bstetrics, *p*ituitary functioning, *q*uasars, *r*ela-tivity, *s*onar, *t*elemetry, *u*ranium mining, *v*i-ruses, *w*ellness, *X*-rays, *y*acht racing, and *z*ool-ogy will have been rewritten.

Before you can absorb and *apply* yesterday's in-take, the explosion of new information floods your receptive capacity. Information only becomes knowledge when it's applied. Constant exposure to the daily information and media shower leaves each of us incapable of ingesting and synthesizing, let alone applying the data, before tomorrow's shower.

The eruption of information in all areas easily renders us overstimulated. The more information you try to ingest, the faster it seems the clock races, and your sense of breathing space is strained.

When the volume of information you believe you need to function exceeds what you can absorb and apply, the result is perpetual frustration. Professor Marshall McLuhan observed that we confront the deluge "with an enormous backlog of outdated mental and psychological responses," and are often left

d
  a
    n
      g
        l
          i
            n
              g.

REPORTING LIVE FROM PARIS

❏ In 1292, the Sorborne Library in Paris housed 1,338 books, most handwritten, representing nearly all of humankind's accumulated knowledge spanning a few thousand years.

❏ In 1992, worldwide, at least 365,000 books are published each year—more than 1,000 a day. Thank you for reading this one!

❏ One edition of the Sunday *New York Times* contains more information items than the typical adult in 1892 was exposed to during his entire life.

❏ Thousands of new magazines and journals were launched in the United States in the last few years. The Harvard Library subscribes to more than 160,000 journals.

❏ All told, more books and articles are published in one day than you could comfortably read in the rest of your life.

Granted, no single individual is exposed to anywhere near the volume of data generated, but the trickle down and spillover effects are phenomenal and unabiding.

Too much information violates our senses and even becomes harmful. As you receive more information, you experience stress, anxiety, even helplessness. Your perception of breathing space is adversely and directly influenced by the more news, information, and details that you ingest, or believe you have to ingest.

It's more so with each passing day that there is no fixed body of knowledge that everyone can be counted on as knowing.

FRESH AIR: Choose to acquire knowledge that supports or interests you, not knowledge that you simply happened to ingest, or think you have to ingest.

The End of the Over-information Era. In ten years or so, smart homes with computers built into the walls, like those on "Star Trek," will become affordable. Such computers will respond to voice commands, offer a completely random-access data base, provide instant simulation through artificial reality, and free us to use information effectively, not be abused by it.

For now, we're stuck in the mire of the over-information era. The best hope to hold off the din is to get to know this sucker as best we can, in all its disguises. If we cannot apply, reflect upon, or, at a minimum, effectively store information, you and I need to guard vigilantly against being deluged with excess data.

FRESH AIR: You *can* become your own information switchboard, by turning off your information receptors for several hours each day. Do not let new information invade your being if it doesn't immediately relate to you, your family, community, or any area of your life, or if it comes after hours.

The Rise of Misinformation. The amount of contradictory information and discrepancies is rising. Annually, more than 40,000 scientific journals publish over 1 million new articles.

"The number of scientific articles and journals published worldwide is starting to confuse researchers, overwhelm the quality-control systems of science, encourage fraud, and distort the dissemination of important findings," says *New York Times* science journalist William J. Broad.

Far too many legislators, regulators, and others *entrusted* to devise the rules that guide the course of society *take shelter in the information overglut by intentionally adding to it*. We are saddled with twenty-eight-page laws that could be stated in two pages, and regulations that contradict themselves every fourth page.

Thus far in our social evolution, these wordcrafters are *not* held accountable for their wordiness. Nevertheless, those who practice to obscure, beware: The insufferable tax you levy on society will soon be recognized for what it is. Your day of reckoning is coming, and faster than you think.

Endless Bombardment. Accuracy and clarity aside, the explosion of information renders us over-informed, but unable to maintain a chronological, let alone a meaningful, context. As an illustration, do you know in what year these historic events occurred, all of which visibly or emotionally impacted our society?

1. Active American military involvement in Vietnam ended?
2. The United States first put a man on the moon?

3. The shuttle *Challenger* exploded in air?
4. The Arab oil embargo resulted in massive lines at U.S. gasoline service stations?
5. The Three Mile Island mishap occurred?

Not knowing the answers (see next page) doesn't reveal a lack of education; rather, you've likely been bombarded with too much data since the early 1970's. By taking in too much, the boundaries that would have aided your recall become blurred.

With such blurring, all events seem as if they are part of one unending eyewitness newscast. Eyewitness news may be interesting, but it does little—if anything—to help you keep events in perspective.

PURE MYTHOLOGY: To not "keep up" is to fall behind.

God forbid, suppose you were in a coma for an entire year. You then awoke with no lingering effects. Two years later, what detriment would you experience for having missed a whole year's exposure to the flood of information you currently encounter?

The answer, for nearly everyone, is a big fat goose egg—none, zero, zed, zilch. Considering your long-term health and well-being, a week, a month, or a year out of the information shower *has no detrimental effect.* If you agree so far, why are you so adamant about attempting to "keep pace"? And why do you feel guilty because you fail?

Except in very specific areas of interest, there is no possibility of keeping pace. There *are*, however, choices to make about *where* you want to focus your energy and attention.

FRESH AIR: Go ahead, make your day. Give yourself permission to go a whole Saturday or Sunday without reading anything.

FRESH AIR: As yet, few people are wise information consumers. At all points, there is only one party who controls the volume, rate, and frequency of information that you're exposed to. That person is you. The notion of "keeping up" is illusory, self-defeating, frustrating, and harmful. The sooner you give it up the better you'll feel.

I would like now to present the third mega-reality, media growth and electronic addiction, in all its glory.

Answers: (1) 1975 (2) 1969 (3) 1986 (4) 1973 (5) 1979

Media Growth and Electronic Addiction

Families don't want to fight over what to watch: 43 percent have at least three television sets.
—JACK NILLES,
NEWSPAPER CORRESPONDENT

As a society, our exposure to the media has increased several hundred percent within a few decades. Yes, Virginia, local channels used to sign off at 11 P.M., before Johnny, before Jay, before Arsenio, and long before CNN. Remember when you had to get up to change the channels? Do you know what teenagers in my town call the remote-control channel device? The godbox.

As population growth and the explosion of information continue unchecked, so, too, does the effect of the mass market on our lives. Certainly, worldwide media coverage provides many benefits. The

rapid spread of democracy in recent years is attrib-
utable in part to people throughout the world seeing
or learning about how other people live and work.

The Proliferation of Messages. As we spend more
and more hours tuned to electronic media, we are
exposed to tens of thousands of messages and images. Similarly, too much food at one sitting, too
much data, in any form, isn't easily ingested.

REPORTING LIVE FROM HOLLYWOOD

- ❑ Three out of five television households own
  VCRs, while the number of movie tickets sold
  and videos rented in the United States each
  exceeded 1 billion annually, starting in 1988.

- ❑ More than 575 motion pictures are produced
  each year compared with an average 175
  twelve years ago. ("So that's why the flicks
  keep changing before I get to the theater!")

- ❑ The average person spends more than eight
  solid years watching electronically how other
  people supposedly live.

- ❑ Twenty years ago, three major networks dom-
  inated television—ABC, NBC, and CBS. Today, well, you know the story. . . . In fact,
  there are now 339 full-power independent
  television stations.

- ❑ Many cable television subscribers receive up

> to 140 television channels, offering more than 72,000 shows per month.
>
> ❏ And for you sports fans, in 1970, no regular-season college basketball games aired on network television. In 1991, more than 1,500 were aired on network or cable television.

I'm not value-judging the effect of TV on society. Many others already have, and it is not my purpose to do so. Besides, you're going to keep watching the same amount you always do!

Regardless of whether you flip the channels, you're subject to an onslaught of issues and images. As Neil Postman, Ph.D., observed in his little-known masterpiece, *Amusing Ourselves to Death: Public Discourse in the Age of Television*, with the three words "and now this . . . ," any TV news anchor is able to hold your attention while shifting gears 180 degrees.

Radio listenership does not lag either. From 5 A.M. to 5 P.M. each weekday in America, listenership far surpasses that of television viewership.

Reporting Live from Radio City Music Hall in New York

> ❏ Since television was first introduced, the number of radio stations has increased tenfold.
>
> ❏ Ninety-seven percent of all households own

an average of five radios (not counting car radios).

❏ On weekdays, 95.2 percent of Americans listen to radio for an average of three hours and fourteen minutes.

❏ Typical salaries for morning shock-talk DJs in major cities are $300,000 to $600,000 per year, plus bonuses.

FRESH AIR: Instead of letting yourself be buffeted by news coverage that skips around the world and changes topics at the speed of "now this . . . ," give a chance to the shows that intelligently cover the issues for more than forty-five seconds each, such as "The MacNeil-Lehrer News Hour," C-Span, "Firing Line," and most shows by Bill Moyers.

They may not be as titillating as coverage on the networks, but you're bound to understand prevailing issues in more depth, and have a better chance of preserving your sense of equilibrium.

FRESH AIR: To better grasp the context of world events, read history, travel, talk to foreigners, and, if so inclined, listen to shortwave broadcasts from other countries (increasingly in English!).

Speak to Me, Anything

We are an anxious society that uses electronics to not feel alone, to evade confronting why we can't seem to get what we want, or to avoid better use of the free hours we say we so earnestly want.

As each breakthrough in communication and entertainment technology is introduced, it is accompanied by predictions of doom for its predecessors. Television was supposed to finish off radio, and VCRs were supposed to do the same to movie theaters. It hasn't happened.

We retain, embrace, and offer rapt attention to all forms of media, and to the devices that transmit them to us. Why else would we make multi-million-dollar celebrities out of buffoon TV meteorologists and morning exercise show hosts?

You can't afford to pay homage to everyone else's fifteen minutes of fame.

The Shrinking Attention Span. Our cultural, *electronic* addiction to the mass media not only inverts our perception of available time; it also diminishes our attention spans. Television and radio news and features grow shorter and shorter to match the fragmented, *decreasing attention spans* of viewers.

TRY THIS: For the next minute, stare at your watch, or if that's too boring, think about something pleasurable you're going to do today. Your perception of the length of a minute will differ vastly from using that minute to listen to the news or read a page from a magazine.

WARNING: The exercise you were going to undertake for a full minute may have just failed.

Our culture is so committed to motion and to information intake that you may be unable to make yourself stare at your watch or simply contemplate for one minute, even when the thought is of something pleasurable!

FRESH AIR: Tomorrow morning, while getting ready for work, rather than switching on the radio or TV, quietly envision how you would like your day to be. Include everything that's important to you— the commute, entering your building or your office, sitting down at your desk, handling tasks, and taking breaks.

Envision interacting with others, going to lunch, conducting or attending meetings, using the phone, finishing up projects, and departing that evening. With this exercise alone, you'll begin to feel a greater sense of control over aspects of your job that you may have considered uncontrollable.

The Rise of Sensationalism

Earlier in this century, to build his newspaper chain and to sell more papers, William Randolph

Hearst used sensationalism to heighten the most mundane of stories. For example, if one of his reporters turned in a story about a dog who got his paw stuck in a sewer grate, Hearst would have the headline changed to read, CANINE TRAPPED IN TUNNEL OF DEATH.

Today, to capture an overstimulated, distracted population, television and other news media rely more and more on sensationalism. It's now ingrained in the nature of broadcasting, and it's hazardous to your breathing space.

With a planet of more than 5 billion people, the media are easily furnished with an endless supply of turmoil for mass transmission. At any given moment, somebody is fomenting violence somewhere. Such turmoil is packaged daily for the evening news.

We are lured with images of crashes, hostages, and natural disasters. We offer our time and rapt attention to each new hostility, scandal, or disaster. Far more people die annually from choking on food than in plane crashes or by guns, but crashes and shootings make for great footage, and play into people's fears. On TV, if it bleeds, it leads.

Your chance of dying from a domestic airplane mishap actually is 1 in 2.6 million. So, you need only be concerned if you fly five flights per week, fifty-two weeks per year, for four or five thousand years.

FRESH AIR: Unless it directly affects you or your community, give up offering any attention, *whatsoever*, to news coverage of spectacular crashes and train wrecks, etc. If you're concerned about reducing the incidence of violent death, learn the Heimlich maneuver or CPR. But puuuleeeeeeease, stop being enthralled by spectacular media coverage of nonimperative events and sensationalized trivia.

Electronic Compression

The average TV scene change in a situation comedy or drama is 3.5 seconds; take out your stopwatch some evening. The media moguls discovered that at that rate, you have to pay attention or you can't keep up.

TV commercials followed suit, and added rock music backdrops, more skits, less straight pitch, and more image creation. In fact, television commercials of five-, ten-, and fifteen-second lengths have largely replaced thirty- and sixty-second commercials.

Studies show that short commercials can be equally as effective as long ones. Thus, you and I are exposed to more penetrating messages in the same interval, if, of course, we don't use the godbox to flip around and pick up ten or twenty other nonrelated images and information tidbits.

The impact of the messages is subtle but powerful. Individual preferences and standards yield to media-imposed values—a mass "keeping up with the Joneses." When you want what others have, you work harder and believe you need to earn more money before feeling you have "made it."

What Does It All Mean?

If you agree that a growing world population, electronically linked by an ever-stronger media industry, ensures that the news and explosion of information will continue to spread, the rest of this chapter may help you maintain perspective.

As more population-related issues,
    information items, and media reports
        compete for your attention, invariably
            you will sense a loss of breathing space.

What's New This Second? Even if your viewership/listenership remains about the same, each day for the rest of your life you will be informed of an increasing number of compelling new issues, social injustices, worthy causes, and late-breaking events, all of which will compete for your attention.

Though your quest to ingest such reports may be worthy, you will not be able to actually sort, classify, or apply more than a few scraps of what you take in, and *you will never be able to "keep up."*

Occasionally, I think that if I pay close attention to the mass media shower, some kind of grand order will emerge that will put everything in context. Then I read about Albert Einstein, who toiled to derive a unified theory of the universe toward the end of his career, but did not succeed.

Likewise, to conclude his brilliant trilogy, Alvin Toffler attempted to develop a social model in

Powershift to predict where we're all heading, but did not.

With the affairs of humankind, there may or may not be some larger order. If there is, it's unlikely you will grasp it by ingesting the mass media barrage. What's dangerous is that with its sensationalized trivia, the mass media overglut obscures fundamental issues that *do* merit the concern of individuals globally, such as preserving the environment.

Meanwhile, broadcasts themselves regularly imply that it is uncivil or immoral not to tune into the daily news—"all the news you need to know," and "we won't keep you waiting for the latest . . ."

It is *not* immoral not to "keep up" with the news that is offered. However, to "tune out"—to turn your back on the world—is not appropriate either. Being more selective in what you give your attention to, and to how long you give it, makes more sense.

FRESH AIR: There is little utility in intellectually resonating with the world's challenges and problems. Pick *one* cause or *one* issue, and take some kind of action *outside* your home. Action is invigorating. Your ability to make a real, if minute, difference will immediately lessen your concerns about attaining some breathing space.

5

The Paper Trail Culture

The biggest problem facing business today is that most managers have too much information. It dazzles them and they don't know what to do with it all.

—LEE IACOCCA, CEO,
CHRYSLER CORPORATION

Imagine staring out the window from the fifth floor of a building and seeing a stack of reports from the ground up to your eye level. This fifty-five-foot-high stack would weigh 660 pounds. *Pulp & Paper* reports that that's the height and weight of paper that Americans annually consume per person.

Similar to too much information, or too many eyewitness reports, having to deal with too much paper, in any form, is going to put a definite crimp in your sense of breathing space.

If you are a white collar worker, the chances are astronomical that controlling the paper flow in your life is a burning issue with you right now. The sea of paper you face is endemic to this society—it's not just you!

American paper consumption per person is twice as much as the British or the Japanese, nine times more than the Russians, and twenty-three times more than the Chinese.

REPORTING LIVE FROM THE PACIFIC NORTHWEST

❏ The documentation for a Boeing 747 weighs more than the plane itself.

❏ Several million pages were printed to document the trials, heats, and finals of the 1988 Summer Olympic competitions in Calgary.

❏ This year, Congress received more than 300 million pieces of mail, up from 15 million in 1970.

❏ Today, 55 million printers are plugged into at least that number of computers, and annually spew out billions of reams of paper. Paperless office, where are you?

❏ Are 18,000 sheets enough? Your four-drawer file cabinet, when full, holds 18,000 pages.

The Direct Mail Glut

The Thoreau Society reports that last year, Henry David Thoreau, who personally has been unable to make any purchases since 1862, received ninety direct mail solicitations at Walden Pond.

Under the existing postal rates in this society, catalog publishers and junk mail producers can miss the target on 98 percent of the attempts and still make a profit—*if only 2 percent of recipients* place an order, direct mailers can score big.

Attempting to sell more, direct mailers send you record amounts of unsolicited mail, more than double what you received in 1978. Meanwhile, regular mail delivery and express mail delivery per capita rise every year.

REPORTING LIVE FROM THE U.S. POSTAL SERVICE IN WASHINGTON

❑ In 1988, 12 billion catalogs were mailed in the United States, up from 5 billion in 1980—equal to fifty catalogs for every man, woman, and child in America.

❑ In the last decade, growth in the total volume of regular, third-class bulk mail (junk mail) was thirteen times faster than growth in the population.

❑ The typical executive receives more than 225 pieces of unsolicited mail each month.

❑ Greenpeace, stalwart protector of the environment, annually sends out 25 million pieces of direct mail.

> ❑ The average person spends a total of eight solid months of his or her life reading junk mail. I *want* those eight months. How about you?

Covering One's Own

It's not simply that we can and do generate the paper, but that we feel important doing it. The funny thing is, we condone each other's overuse of paper. Our unarticulated credo has become:

> **I PHOTOCOPY, THEREFORE I AM.**

Or "I fax, therefore I am," or "Have laser printer, will make dozens of copies." No birth control for reprints—just endless reproduction, a world imaging itself. Memoranda infinitum.

Why is documentation, like circulating a copy to your boss, so critical to this culture? Because everyone is afraid of getting his derrière roasted! We live in a culture of fear, not like some martial law dictatorships, but a form of fear nonetheless. "If I cannot account, I cannot prove, or defend myself."

Attempting to contain what seems unmanageable, public and private organizations create paper accounting systems. These accounting systems go by such names as federal income taxes, deed of trust, car loan, etc. Sure, accounting is necessary, but why so complicated? Because in the era of over-information, overdocumentation is regarded as appropriate protection. Such systems provide temporary relief and some sense of order. Usually, however, they become ingrained and immovable, while creating more muddle.

Corporate cultures subject their employees and constituents to substantial paperwork. Firing an incompetent worker requires reams of documentation. Similarly, job promotions, client billing, investment analysis, and fund raising require voluminous paperwork. Corporate paper flow itself accounts for 70 percent of all corporate activity today.

Your Own Private Paper Glut

Because your own paper glut is something that you continually confront, in many ways it is most hazardous to your sense of breathing space.

You can shield yourself for stretches from the other mega-realities, but those piles of paper on your desk and around your office—gadzooks! (Help is on the way in chapters 10 through 13.)

Since about 80 percent of papers retained in office environments are never used, you're probably holding on to five times what you need, and your ability to find and use what you need becomes difficult and requires additional effort.

FRESH AIR: Clear the in-bins of your mind and your desk. Regard each piece of paper that enters your personal kingdom as a potential mutineer, rebel, or disloyal subject. Every piece of paper has to earn its keep and remain worthy of your retention. Were it to speak, it would have to convey immediately its value to you. If it could not, it has to volunteer for recycling (where it just might come back to you someday!).

An Over-abundance
of Choices

The difficulty in life is in the choice.
—GEORGE MOORE,
19TH CENTURY IRISH WRITER

In the mid-1980's movie *Moscow on the Hudson*, actor Robin Williams portrays a Russian defector who settles in New York. He goes to the supermarket one day to buy some coffee.

The markets he knew in Moscow were small, poorly lit, and ill stocked. The Manhattan supermarket is dazzling. The display of coffee simply overwhelms him—there is instant, freeze dried, dark brew, flavored, Colombian, decaffeinated, and espresso in dozens of boxes, cans, and jars of different sizes and different colors.

Confronted with a sudden, vast array of choices, his reaction is perfectly reasonable under the circumstances. He has an anxiety attack, faints, pitches forward, and end up knocking over the whole display.

When I tell this story during my speeches, it invariably gets a chuckle or two. Yet, you and I are being besieged in the same way, and each day we suffer the same anxiety, if imperceptibly.

In his 1970 book *Future Shock*, Alvin Toffler predicted that we would become slaves to an overabundance of choices. Toffler described how more choices inhibit action, resulting in greater anxiety and the perception of less freedom and less time.

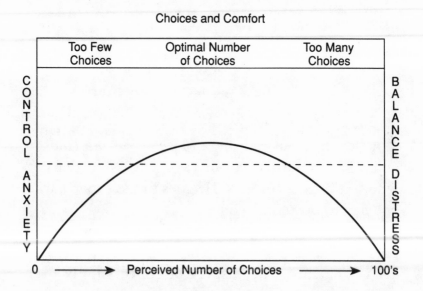

Choices and Comfort

Having an abundance of choices seems a blessing—a benefit of living in a democratic society. Like too much of everything else, however, having too many choices is harmful to your breathing space and results not only in increased time expenditure, but also in a mounting form of exhaustion.

The Mating Game

Having too many choices often leads to no selection at all. In one city after another, you hear the same lament among singles: "There are no eligible men in this town," or "This town is a bust when it comes to women."

Today, however, if you're in search of a mate, or simply a date, the reality is that there have *never* been more potential partners for you, in every community, of either sex, at all ages.

There are so many choices that, for some, choosing is all but impossible. For others, the mating process seems too burdensome, in the face of everything else they're confronting.

What if you were forced to meet your future mate among a fixed population of, say, 10,000 people in a small town nearby. Could you do it? You're darned right you could.

What if you *had* to confine your selection to those potential partners you already knew? Could you find someone with whom you could be happy? Probably, you very well could. So, why can't you choose among hundreds of thousands of people? Among a sea of excuses, the predominant answer is too many choices.

Let's change the scene. Suppose you're stuck in a small beach town on a chilly Saturday afternoon when it starts pouring rain. You duck into the nearest building, the town library. The library is so tiny it only has one book case. You almost laugh.

For some reason, all the shelves except one are barren. That shelf contains six books. Although you're not familiar with any of them, you start thumbing through the volumes.

Now for the $10 million lotto jackpot: Somewhere among those six books, can you find a chapter that can hold your interest, an engrossing character, or a captivating passage? Of course you can.

Why, then, do you so often ignore the books on your shelf at home? You know, the ones you have been meaning to read for eight years! Too many choices of both books to read and other things to do could be the reason.

FRESH AIR: Periodically, the sweetest choice is choosing from what you already have, choosing to actually have what you've already chosen.

No Breaks

Daily, each of us is confronted surreptitiously by the pressing, awesome responsibility to keep choosing:

> Rob H. gets up on Saturday morning at 8:45. His wife is a real estate agent and has already left to meet a client. Rob has a choice of five cereals and four coffees, breakfast at the fast-food restaurant six blocks away, or not eating. After breakfast, Rob may go to his office in town to finish some work—it would be nice to get a jump on Monday. Or he may try to unplug a clogged sink. He'd call a plumber, but they want $48 just to come over.

As he explores the kitchen shelves, Rob thinks about how he has not been to the health club in weeks and would like to swim. However, the first football game will be on at noon and he doesn't want to miss the kickoff. Settling for some cold cereal, Rob remembers that Dave, a coworker, needs help moving this weekend.

The newspaper contains a long feature article on a television actor who lost twenty-four pounds in six weeks. Rob reads about two-thirds of the article, and then turns to another section. The closest shopping mall is having a mall-wide sale, and it looks as if it might be worth a ride over there.

He reads a couple more items while finishing breakfast. Around 9:30, he decides to go to the gym, but before getting ready, he notices the clogged sink and begins tinkering with it. Fifty minutes later, Rob is still puttering with the sink. The problem is worse, and he gives up.

Frustrated, he heads for the gym, but hurries back not to miss the kickoff. He picks up his mail on the way in. There are a few bills, some advertising fliers, and, unsolicited, a new credit card. He wonders, "Is this worth keeping?"

It is noon on the first of his two days off. Rob already feels a bit anxious. By Sunday night, he'll be exhausted and won't know why. On Monday morning, he will commute to work, anxious rather than rested, and only partially prepared to be productive.

Rob feels as if he is always behind. Is there a little of Rob in you? Or a lot? Amidst our multioption society, even minor decisions hobble a surprising number of people. In one survey of 1,000 Americans, more than 50 percent had trouble *choosing a doctor, a vacation spot, or clothes from their closet* for a special occasion.

Let's revisit Rob and see how his Saturday might go, given his awareness that too many choices can be hazardous to his breathing space:

Rob gets up at 8:45 and decides to have cold cereal with milk, while reading the paper. At 9:30, the plumber is coming over to fix the downstairs sink. Rob waits until the plumber is finished. Then Rob departs for the health club at around 10:20. He'd like to make it back for the football game at noon, but has decided that it's more important for him to get a good workout, and to take a leisurely shower. On Friday, he had to decline helping a coworker move this weekend—Rob knew that he needed some time to take it easy.

On the way back home, Rob picks up the mail. Rather than read it now, he puts it neatly in the corner of his desk in the den. It's 12:30 P.M. now and he flips on the television.

He watches the football game until halftime, then goes to the den and handles the mail.

He's back to see the second half. His team loses! Afterward, Rob decides to take an afternoon nap, rather than watch the next game. His wife won't be home until 4:30, and dinner is at 5:30 this evening—so why not give his body some well-deserved rest?

REPORTING LIVE FROM THE SAFEWAY IN YOUR NEIGHBORHOOD

❑ The supermarket glut: Gorman's *New Product News* reports that in 1978, the typical supermarket carried 11,767 items. By 1987, that figure had risen to an astounding 24,531 items—more than double in nine years.

❑ More than 45,000 other products were introduced during those years, but failed.

❑ Elsewhere in the supermarket, Hallmark Cards now offers cards for 105 familial relationships. My goodness!

❑ Currently, more than 1,260 varieties of shampoo are on the market. Seventy-five different types of exercise shoes are now available, each with scores of variations in style.

❑ More than 2,000 skin care products are availabe currently.

As more specialty foods, cuisines, dietary supplements, and nonfood items are introduced, the typical supermarket soon will carry 40,000 items. Will there be room? Yes. Each product line carried will occupy a lesser amount of shelf space.

FRESH AIR: No matter how many items the supermarket stocks, you can continue to buy what you have always bought, tuning out the rest. That could get a little tedious. You like to try new things? Then, on each trip to the supermarket, make a goal of exploring one new area. It could be in the meats, fruits, cheeses, frozen foods, whatever.

If you shop once a week, in the course of the next year you will have tried at least 50 new products without expending mental effort or consternation in the process.

Toffler had it right when he advocated not engaging in low-level decisions. If the same toothbrush is available with a red, blue, yellow, or white handle, and it is all the same to you, just grab the one that is closest or take the one that the clerk hands to you.

FRESH AIR: Whenever you catch yourself making a low-level decision, consider: Does this really make a difference? Get in the habit of making only a few decisions a day—the ones that count.

The Tyranny of Too Many Choices

So it goes with automobiles, VCRs, stereos, camcorders, telephones, answering machines, cameras, sailboats, fax machines, silverware, china, baby strollers, and hair dryers.

So it also goes with frequent flyer programs, investments, long distance telephone service, medical insurance, retirement options. The choices mount, the rules and regulations take longer to read, and are harder to understand.

Awareness, interest, purchase, consumption, and maintenance of these products is draining. Every new product you are exposed to pilfers a portion of your day, however meager, with a predictable cumulative effect. How many impossible VCR-type manuals are you willing to wade through?

FRESH AIR: Consider the value of any product, service, or plan as twofold: (1) the intended benefit and (2) *the ease with which you can understand, receive, and enjoy those benefits.* If it doesn't provide both, don't buy it. There will be plenty of other options available, believe me!

FRESH AIR: Produce your own specifications list of exactly what you want in a product or service. For example, in buying an electric razor, you might choose portability, light weight, attractive shape, a warrantee, etc. Copy this list and show it to a few prospective vendors to see what they propose. Add any other features they suggest. Now, compose your final list and re-present it to several vendors to see how they match up with your wants and needs. This approach helps reduce confusion, saves time, and helps avoid selection errors.

Or take two aspirin, get some rest, and find the appropriate issue of *Consumer Reports* or *Consumer's Digest* in the morning.

7

Running in Place, or the Alligator Who Ate Its Tail

No man in a hurry is quite civilized.
—WILL DURANT, HISTORIAN
AND AUTHOR

Don't flip ahead yet!

The combined effect of the five mega-realities accelerates clock chasing, although the symptoms are not always acknowledged as such. Speed bumps in parking lots weren't necessary years ago.

Let's explore the ill-advised practice of engaging in simultaneous activities, such as reading while eating. You may read while eating alone for company, not because of time pressure. Nevertheless, when you read while you eat, or vice versa, *neither activity is fully experienced,* and you perceive that the hour is passing more quickly.

Writer Marta Vogel observes, "Early man looked at his food to make sure it was dead and that it didn't have any bugs in it. But 20th century man no longer looks at the food itself; he looks at the package. Corporate America discovered that man could become addicted to package reading in almost any situation."

Recognizing our craving for information, advertisers provide enticing product packaging. The average cereal box contains about 2,000 words, equal to eight pages of this book. Vogel says, "Generic products [of the same quality as mid-level brands] were offered with the knowledge that no one might buy wordless cardboard and risk an attack of package deprivation."

Package deprivation? Hmmm. It probably comes as no surprise to you that more than half our population wears clothes or accessories designed with slogans and messages on them.

FRESH AIR: Attraction to labeling and package copy further robs you of breathing space. So do clothes, yours or others', with messages on them. Minute bits of extraneous data do have a cumulative impact. You deserve a real break today. Eat some *nutritious food*, with people dressed in clothes with no printed messages, and with no reading material in sight.

Other symptoms of running in place abound— not only while eating. Do you attempt to think, converse, study, or even make love with distractions? Do you go through the motions of attempting to concentrate with office noise? Do you awake by alarm clock?

Do three square meals and sufficient sleep mean anything to you? Are long-standing hobbies no longer of interest to you? Do old friends only merit an occasional phone call?

Do you attempt to talk while watching television? Do you "need" to wind down before bed in front of the TV? Can you even sit in front of it without turning it on?

FRESH AIR: Telltale signs of being too busy:

If you're too busy to enjoy your life, you're too busy.

If you're too busy to stay calm, you're too busy.

If you're too busy to stay in shape, you're too busy.

If you're too busy to see your friends, you're too busy.

If you think that someday you'll "catch up" in all these areas, you are living under a delusion.

Low-Quality Leisure

True leisure—enjoying rewarding activity free from work and preoccupation with work—is a necessary component of a balanced life. When the shift between pressure-filled activity and true leisure is abrupt, the quality of your leisure is likely to suffer. Is your leisure force-fitted between frenzied activities? Are you living a life of symbolic success, i.e., you have a nice home and salary but you can't enjoy either?

Strains of the work week tend to make you place great emphasis on your weekends and other days off. You hope to relax, but the pressure is enormous, and often you can't rest even when you've got the hours to do so.

Constant time pressure invariably leads to anxiety and guilt about where and to what you give your attention. Too often, quality time is a lie. Many fathers' weekend encounters with their children *is scheduled*, if it exists at all. "Dad never plays with us anymore."

The pressured individual feels guilty both doing too much and doing too little. "Could I have done more?" "Should I have done otherwise?" Even when blessed with leisure, your mind may not be free to enjoy it.

Parents are concerned about how long they spend with their kids. Spouses feel guilty about periods spent away from each other. Pressed and frazzled by the onslaught of responsibilities, more couples are finding it exhausting to have to "be" with one another—to converse, empathize, respond—reports *Working Woman*. Let's face it, being very busy is a form of escapism.

Annually, the number of families headed by a single adult, usually female, is growing, placing inordinate strains on working individuals with children. Families with two incomes have more money and spend more, but invariably experience great time pressure. In any case, a cultural inability to relax dogs us and negates many benefits leisure could provide if we would only relax and enjoy it.

This, in turn, influences the quality of your work day. Even as more labor-saving technologies and communication technologies are introduced, and your output and efficiency rise, your expectations directly increase. You become less satisfied with yourself for not doing more.

Human Doings. The feeling of no breathing space can quickly pervade all aspects of your life, diminish your happiness, and eliminate any *joie de vivre*. The cycle can get exceedingly vicious.

Lacking a balance between work and play, responsibility and respite, "getting things done" becomes the end-all. You function like a human doing instead of a human being.

You begin to link successfully executing the items on your growing "to do" list with feelings of worthiness. As the list keeps growing longer, the lingering sense of more to do infiltrates your sense of harmony and self-acceptance.

FRESH AIR: When your days on earth are over and the big auditor in the sky examines the ledger of your life, she'll be upset if you *didn't* take enough breaks and vacations, and if you didn't enjoy yourself.

Institutional Impediments

Commonplace working conditions such as those cited below exacerbate pressure on the job, which diminishes the quality of life away from the job:

- ❏ Corporate-sponsored workaholism—found to be at epidemic levels in several studies.
- ❏ Lack of mentoring. Formally or informally established mentor/protégé links are actually rare. Guidance saves time.
- ❏ Working under unnecessary pressure. Constantly time-pressed managers do less planning, while requiring of others that more tasks be completed quickly. Workers constantly under pressure bring it home with them.
- ❏ Inadequate or nonexistent day care—the shame of otherwise "modern" corporations.

People on their first or second job feel intense pressure to make the grade, while often being un-schooled as to how to pace themselves. Workers of all ages who assume increasing responsibility often feel pressure unknown earlier in their careers.

Entrepreneurs work long and hard with little leisure, and, for most, with significant stress. The entrepreneurial life has been heralded and miscon-strued, and sensationalized as well.

PURE MYTHOLOGY: "Work expands so as to fill the time allotted for its completion." Not anymore, Mr. Parkinson! Not in the era of over-information. Parkinson's Law is hereby repealed.

If I may be so bold:

DAVIDSON'S LAW: "Items competing for one's attention expand so as to fill the time and hinder work allocated for completion."

FRESH AIR: You are whole and complete right now. Everything on your "to-do" list, even at the workplace, is undertaken at your option. You *are not* your tasks; they don't define you and they don't constrain you.

Self-Imposed Impediments

Regardless of your type of employment and the pressure the company puts on you, your own behaviors and attitudes can diminish the quality of your leisure, if not deplete it altogether. Do any of the following describe you to a T?

❑ Unrealistic expectations—why shouldn't I be able to achieve ABC . . .
❑ Overcommitting, or having unrealistic goals— leads to frequent clock-chasing.
❑ Overachieving—the desire to achieve more and more swallows days and weeks.
❑ Living on credit—buy, work harder, pay.
❑ Preoccupied—not living in the present, which fortifies the constant perception of no time.

❑ Overanticipating—a trap to miss the present and cause disappointment over the leisure that is available.

FRESH AIR: On a deeply felt personal level, recognize that from now on, you will be subjected to an ever-increasing number of items competing for your attention. Each of the five mega-realities will get far worse, if indeed they ever get better. It's couth to unburden your calendar! You cannot handle everything, nor is making the attempt desirable.

Recognize, with the clarity of death, that your life is finite; you can no longer wistfully intake the daily deluge and expect to achieve balance. You cannot submissively yield to the din, and settle for living your life in what's left over after each day's onslaught. You alone need to make sensible choices regarding what is best ignored and what merits your attention.

Let's turn now to hand tools that will help you achieve breathing space and activate your potential to take control, starting with the rudimentary and moving to the magnificent.

HAND TOOLS

8

What Fills Your Days and Why?

You will never find time for anything.
If you want it you must make it.
—CHARLES BUXTON
19TH CENTURY BRITISH POLITICIAN

My sister Nancy is a behavioral psychologist who works with clients in therapy to determine, among other things, how they spend their days. "It's a significant clue to whatever type of dysfunctioning they may be experiencing."

Tell me how you spend your time, and I'll tell you what your troubles are.

A wheel stuck in the mud, spinning fast, certainly represents rapid motion. Yet the car is not moving. Are your days filled with activity but not the experiences and accomplishments you'd like to enjoy?

When you examine the broad canvas of your life, interesting surprises often surface. What you say is important to you isn't on your schedule. What you say you dislike is where you expend energy.

Busy or not, everyone has 168 hours a week. I checked. One way or another, everyone fills them. Consider the cumulative amount of years you spend doing various activities.

Any activity consuming thirty minutes of your day consumes *two solid years of your life.* Say that again? During a work life of forty-eight years (between ages twenty-two and seventy), any activity that you engage in for an average of thirty minutes each day consumes one complete year of your life.

(½ hr in 24 hours) = (½ yr in 24 years) =
(1 yr in 48 years)

The realization that what you do for only thirty minutes on a daily basis costs you one solid year in the course of your adult life is simple, yet profound. Obviously, there are some things you would not or could not give up, and it is silly to apply this arithmetic to activities such as personal hygiene.

Nevertheless, you have a new perspective for viewing what you do that can aid you in eliminating activities that do not support you. Especially *in this society, in this era,* it also underscores the importance of taking control—looking for new ways of accomplishment and questioning your routines.

Reading the paper each morning need not be abandoned. Watching the eleven o'clock news every night is okay if it's *your* continuing choice. Merely recognize that you are making a decision that could affect your breathing space.

Elliott feels anxious when he doesn't keep up with the latest news. While driving, he frequently tunes to the all-news radio station. He doesn't read the paper daily, but he always scans the front page. After work, he catches the evening news or the late-night report.

Elliott is caught in a trap. He is experiencing anxiety associated with the fallacy of keeping posted. It is of no consequence for Elliott to hear daily reports on a midwest mayor being investigated for corruption, or a Third World leader clinging to power, or the four-alarm fire last night in the next town.

Still, as the years pass, Elliott consumes thousands of hours of his life by ingesting such information and being buffeted by the other mega-realities . . . while not accomplishing what he wants and feeling as if he has no breathing space.

Looking Beyond. If lack of breathing space has been a lingering issue for you, look beyond routine, ritual, and victimization to ownership and responsibility for what *is* occurring in your life.

Ritual is routine behavior that is comfortable but outmoded and unrewarding—such as opening all the mail you receive.

Victimization is believing that circumstances or others cause your lack of breathing space. It's continuing to act powerless rather than taking responsibility. (My boss, spouse, father, mother, kids, in-laws, neighbor, landlord, adviser, clergy; or the president, governor, newspaper/magazine columnist, or the devil makes me do it. . . .)

Ownership is accepting full responsibility for what occurs in your life.

It's sad, but every season some high school or college athlete gives up all his breathing space and dies during a physical workout that proves to be too strenuous. Yet what coach wants any of his players to die?

At work, are you dying a little more each season, laboring under a delusion? What's missing is the coach and players, or managers and their staffs, getting together and discussing the boundaries of the relationship, including expectations, reasonable work loads, and limitations.

What Are You Busy About?

Can you imagine Mahatma Gandhi or Martin Luther King, Jr. getting up in the morning and lamenting about all the things he wanted to accomplish that day, or week? Indeed, can you envision anyone of major accomplishment attempting to proceed in life following someone else's priorities?

Can you picture anyone of lasting achievement

engaging in personally hazardous sleep patterns, talking faster, or buying speed-listening tapes? A few years back, when TV commercials with John Moschitta (the speed talker) aired, I know of people who recoiled in their seats. It was that stressful to listen.

Playing games with your body or flooding your senses is the prescription for trouble, not accomplishment—and certainly not breathing space.

If you can look beyond your own routines and rituals, beyond feelings of victimization, your quest becomes one of taking several days and deciding what's important to you. This is intensely personal and can be genuinely rewarding.

The happiest people I know identify and keep identifying what matters to them and then allocate their efforts accordingly. If employed by others and assigned what to do, they are fortunate to be able to make their assignments among their priorities.

These happy souls are able to break free from collective, cultural images of success and be guided by their own choices. Great leaders in society fit this mold. All else eventually leads to some form of internal conflict:

> Sheila is frequently under pressure and many days "stressed out" before noon. She believes her condition is due to her job and factors beyond her control. For Sheila, every day is a battle against the clock.

> Mitch is locked in his own time and income trap. He is afraid to change jobs and stays

rooted to a company that under-values his contribution. So he complains at home, works harder, and becomes a corporate eunuch.

Like Sheila and Mitch, many people will endure years and years with little breathing space, but will not sit down and decide what merits action and attention, and what does not.

Others cling to old world notions of attempting to stay on top of everything. If you are experiencing any of the following, you are in a malfunctioning mode, which indicates inefficiency and a strained sense of breathing space:

❑ Constantly shortchanging the most important tasks.
❑ Attempting to do everything yourself.
❑ Feeling closed in, cramped for space.
❑ Having piles stack up.
❑ Having too many interruptions to concentrate.
❑ Always being late.

Malfunctions can be short- or long-term in duration. Everyone experiences recurring short malfunctions. Short often becomes long—a hazardous situation.

Paying Lip Service to Yourself. Do you identify something as important to you and then give it no energy? Do other lesser items get much more of your attention? If so, chances are you haven't identified

what's important to you; you only have vague notions.

Bill says he values seeing his parents often,
but he only makes the thirty-six-mile round-
trip once every couple of months.

Carolyn says enjoying weekends is important
to her, but she's worked six Saturdays in a
row.

What *Is* Important to You

Making and reaffirming choices about what *is*
important and how you would like to allocate your
resources are crucial. You need to make your choices
away from the rabble, and to acknowledge the fixed
components of your existence:

❑ Youth, young adulthood, and middle age are fi-
nite.
❑ Your productive work life is finite.
❑ Change is guaranteed.
❑ Life is finite; death is guaranteed. Trust me on
this one.

The choices confronting most individuals often
come down to the same few issues: career advancement versus a happy home life; income goals versus
income needs; and social-, peer-, or employment-
induced priorities versus individual wants or needs.

Potential Priority Headings:

Personal: health, welfare, finances, autonomy, intellect, interests, recreation, love, sexual fulfillment.

Family: health, welfare, lifestyle, children's education, recreation, enrichment.

Friends, relatives: health, welfare.

Neighborhood, community, region: appearance, prosperity, schools, roads, institutions.

Country, fellow citizens, government: security, quality of life, freedoms, pursuit of happiness, opportunity, justice.

Fellow human beings: freedom, education, security, welfare, nourishment.

Planet: ecological system, resources, animal and plant life, vitality.

The things most meaningful to you in life are, by definition, your priorities. Priorities are broad elements of life. They often become misplaced somewhere within your daily high-wire balancing act.

It is wise to have only a few priorities. If you have too many, you're not likely to respect each of them. At some point, too many priorities become paradoxical—only a few concerns *can* be of priority.

In establishing your priorities, I suggest the following:

❑ List everything that is important or that you wish to accomplish. Initially, overpick, go crazy.

- ❏ Go back and assess your list. Eliminate the nice but, on second inspection, not so important items.
- ❏ Combine any items that are similar in nature. Having too many priorities leads to frustration and despair, similar to what you've got now.
- ❏ Rewrite, redefine, or restructure any of your choices. If you're not sure of an item, feel free to delete it.
- ❏ Put your list away for another day, then review it.
- ❏ Delete, combine, or rethink any of the items remaining. If something seems less important, drop it. *You can't afford the responsibility of more priorities than you can support.*
- ❏ Complete your list, for now—priorities can change.

Here are examples of priorities you might choose:

"Providing for the education of my children."
"Achieving financial independence."
"Maintaining my loving, happy marriage."
"Working for world peace."

Your priorities may change radically as years pass. They are always based on deeply felt needs or desires, usually representing challenging but ultimately rewarding choices.

FRESH AIR: To get to know someone better, ask him what his life's priorities are. Ask your spouse tonight. Ask yourself.

Your Priority Card

For maximum benefit, I suggest writing your priorities on small business-size cards. Keep one in your wallet, one in your appointment book, and one in your car.

Read your priorities list as often as you can. Reading your list frequently contributes to your sensation of breathing space—it's invigorating when you're actively supporting what you've chosen as important.

It isn't overkill to review a list of your life's priorities EVERY DAY, in light of the overglut you're subject to on all sides. In fact, it is a superior approach to enjoying breathing space.

Supporting Your
Priorities

I go at what I am about as if there was
nothing else in the world for the time
being.
　　　　　—CHARLES KINGSLEY, 19TH
　　　　　　CENTURY ENGLISH AUTHOR

It's one thing to choose your priorities; it's another
to maintain the integrity of your selections. Being
true to your priorities requires setting goals. Far too
often, advice on goal-setting fails to establish the
fundamental connection of goals to larger priorities.

A goal is a statement that is specific about what
you intend to accomplish and when. All the goal-
setting and attainment you ever hoped for, however,
won't bring you breathing space if the goals don't
support your chosen priorities. You'll be spinning
your wheels, rather like employing time manage-

ment while being unaware of the mega-realities that dominate our era and our lives.

To further distinguish priorities from goals: Priorities are the handful of things in your life or career that are important to you. Goals support priorities. Your goals can change as old ones are accomplished and, of course, if some of your life priorities change.

Here are some well-constructed goal statements:

"to work out for forty-five minutes, three sessions weekly, starting today." (Priority: staying healthy.)

"to increase my annual income to $53,000 next year." (Priority: achieving financial independence.)

"to eliminate all nuclear weapon stockpiles by January 1, 1997." (Priority: having peace on earth.)

You can use the same procedure for choosing priorities when choosing goals. The major difference is that each goal has to support a priority, and each priority is supported by at least one goal.

Here are some poorly set goals. Can you tell why?

"to sell as much as I can in the next six months."

"to complete the renovation of the vacation property."

"to be the best employee in the division."

They lack specifics and target dates. Imprecision in goal-setting leads to missed goals. Especially in the over-information era, where distractions grow on trees and on your desk, your goals need to be well set.

Goals may change. A goal that was necessary and appropriate yesterday may suddenly no longer be valid. It's important to establish a few well-chosen goals in support of your priorities, but you also need to recognize that the nature of your responsibilities and interests is going to shift.

FRESH AIR: Study the most successful people in your industry or profession. Most of them are confident, low-anxiety people with clear priorities and goals. They know they can't do their best when they are continually chasing the clock and not making the effort to determine what represents their best moves.

Goal Reinforcement

If you've ever read the comic strip "Cathy," picture this—Cathy has a list on her bulletin board that reads:

- ❑ Clean bedroom.
- ❑ Send thank-you letter.
- ❑ Call Ellen.
- ❑ Visit upholstery store.
- ❑ Write book.

It's easy enough to set a goal, but another thing to stick to it. To support your commitments, here are some reinforcement techniques:

The Calendar Block-back or Back-to-front Method. Assures that a goal will be achieved and milestones reached by using the monthly calendar. Here's how it works. Start from the deadline by which a goal is to be completed. Then, plot the subtasks and activities that you need to undertake from the due date back to the present day.

In other words, proceed in reverse, using the monthly calendar to establish realistic, interim dates that reflect available resources, vacations, holidays, weekends and other off hours, reasonable output levels.

By using the calendar block-back method, you can determine that if, for example, subtask two in pursuit of goal X was accomplished two days late, then the whole project will be two days late unless immediate action is taken.

Contract with Yourself. Author Dennis Hensley describes what he calls Advancement by Contract. "A contract takes precedence over everything else." He suggests carefully selecting three to five major

---

SELF-INITIATED CONTRACT

I, _____, agree to accomplish each of the following items on or before _____ and hereby do formally contract myself to these purposes.

These goals are challenging, but reasonable, and I accept them willingly.

A. _____

B. _____

C. _____

Signature: _____ Date_____

DH © 1983

goals, in support of your priorities, and then signing a contract that aids you in reaching these goals. "Once under contract, you would have to succeed by a preselected date or else face the consequences of defaulting on the contract."

Hensley recommends reviewing your goals and listing as many benefits to be gained as you can by achieving each one. Next, write them into a contract (example, page 80) and make three copies of it. Keep the original and look at it each day. Give one copy each to your spouse, a coworker, and a friend.

Have Somebody Waiting for Your Project. Related to the above, when someone is waiting for your work, the probability increases that you deliver on schedule.

Without putting any extra pressure on yourself, you can create a situation to suit your own needs by appointing a prod who lets you know you are not the only one seeking completion.

> Jennifer discovered that by telling her mother about her school project, her mother's interest in seeing it before Jennifer took it to school served as a spur to completion.

Contrived Compliance—Put $2,000 in an Escrow Fund. If you don't complete your predetermined goal on schedule, your spouse gets the money.

Here are seven more techniques to help you reach your goals:

❏ Visualize the goal. Each day, see yourself having completed the goal. Fantasy helps.

❏ Reward systems. Set up a series of small rewards for yourself as you complete each step or phase in the overall pursuit of your goal.

❏ Laminate, post prominently. As with your priorities, strategically post your goals as a constant reminder.

❏ Affirm. Each morning when you rise, repeat a statement of what you intend to accomplish.

❏ Affiliate. Join others who have a similar goal.

❏ Condition your environment. Surround yourself with what supports your goal (more on conditioning in other chapters).

❏ Remind yourself of what you want. When I find myself straying from course, I often say, "Okay, Jeff, you said you wanted to accomplish this, didn't you?"

Barriers to Goal Attainment

What diminishes your chance of attaining goals?

❏ Having a poor time frame. Picking goals that are too challenging for the available hours, days or weeks available.

❏ Being under-resourced. Selecting a goal without having the tools, money, or proper support.

❏ Operating in a nonsupportive environment. Unforeseen obstacles are always a possibility. Once such obstacles are uncovered, reevaluate the original goal, then recommit to your new choice.

❑ Losing sight of goals or larger priorities. Letting the information overglut obscure your view of the big picture.

❑ Lacking perspective. From peak to peak, mountains don't look too far apart. In the valley between them, the next peak looks farther away, even while you are moving closer toward it.

❑ Confusing priorities with goals. "To have good health" is a priority. To support this priority, you would select specific goals, such as taking vitamins every day, or going to three exercise classes per week, etc.

❑ Following rituals. As previously cited, it consumes time while offering little support toward goals and priorities. Most rituals require a greater investment than their contribution presently warrants. For example: needing two cups of coffee to get started or waiting until the top of the hour, rather than starting a few minutes before.

Some opening-exercise rituals, like arranging your pencils, may help you to be productive, just as the ritual of brushing your teeth helps prevent cavities. The pencils *may* be in your way. Problem rituals are those that have become dinosaurs.

We all engage in useful rituals, which remain in force beyond their usefulness, like Lady Macbeth obsessed with washing her hands. Early in your career, it probably made sense to open all your own mail. Now that you manage a department of twenty-eight people, it no longer makes sense, but you still do it because you've always done it. Haphazard ingestion of data is insidious.

All told, outmoded ritual behavior is among the greatest obstacles to achieving goals and to heightening your sense of breathing space.

Starting Right Where You Are

There cannot be a crisis next week. My
schedule is already full.
—HENRY KISSINGER, FORMER
U.S. SECRETARY OF STATE

The biggest impediment to assisting people in choosing priorities and goals is getting them enthusiastic enough to break inertia. What if it were possible to select goals that supported two priorities? That certainly would streamline your tasks. Below is one way to accomplish such a feat.

1. List your priorities in abbreviated form along the chart top and down the side as indicated.
2. Place an *X* where the same priority intersects with itself. All other boxes are areas in which to write goals.
3. Now the challenge. If Priority B (Pr B) is

enriching your child's education, and Priority C is taking her to Europe, what goal could you choose to support both B and C?

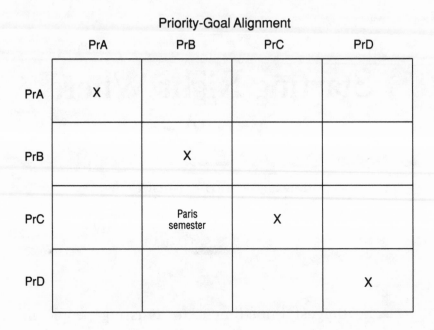

Priority-Goal Alignment

	PrA	PrB	PrC	PrD
PrA	X			
PrB		X		
PrC		Paris semester	X	
PrD				X

Yes—the goal of getting your daughter enrolled in a semester-in-Paris program for her junior year would kill the proverbial two birds with one stone.

With a larger version of the chart, you can list several possible goals that may support dual priorities. Be creative in filling in this chart. You can always reject ideas later. Here is how Ed C. completed one portion of the chart:

Ed's priorities are to (A) take early retirement and (B) start a business of his own. The goal that supports both priorities is to take two evening courses on entrepreneurship so that he can be ready to start within one month of retirement on September 15:

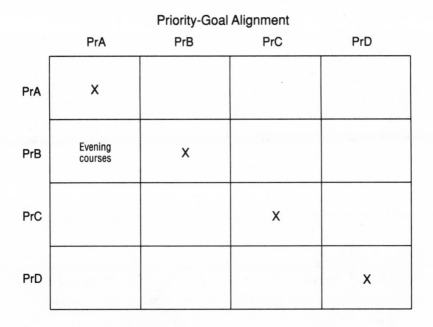

Priority-Goal Alignment

	PrA	PrB	PrC	PrD
PrA	X			
PrB	Evening courses	X		
PrC			X	
PrD				X

Officially stated, Ed's goal is to enroll in two evening courses at the local community college this summer in preparation for his October 15 entrepreneurial debut. More often than not, you'll be able to select goals that serve two priorities.

Margaret, age twenty-eight, is a single parent with four priorities: (A) Achieve financial independence; (B) Finish her degree; (C) Have more of a social life; (D) Have a long and healthy life. Here is how she chose goals in her own words that supported multiple priorities:

Priority-Goal Alignment

	A	B	C	D
A	X	Only take classes I pay for! No more student loans!		
B	Get a degree that will enhance my career, not prepare me for low-wage employment.	X	Take "fun" classes, along with academia, where I can meet people of similar interests.	
C		Balance classes, work, leisure time.	X	Do active things with people; get out of "movie and pizza" ritual.
D		Include courses on nutrition and physical activity.	Join a walking or hiking club.	X

Milestone Charts

Establishing milestones for the completion of the goals you've chosen is an easy way to maintain command of the sequencing and progress toward

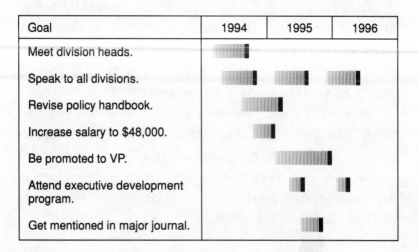

Goal	1994	1995	1996
Meet division heads.			
Speak to all divisions.			
Revise policy handbook.			
Increase salary to $48,000.			
Be promoted to VP.			
Attend executive development program.			
Get mentioned in major journal.			

established goals. On the job, accomplishing goals is usually a given—deadlines have been imposed from above or from the marketplace. However, milestones are also a useful tool for monitoring progress toward personal goals.

The milestone chart portrays each goal, including starting date, interim points, and ending date (if applicable), by years, months, weeks, or days. Many software applications can be used.

Unlike the would-be dieter who is always going to start next week, your campaign begins the moment your milestone chart calls for commencing the activity plotted.

A common weakness of capable people is to underestimate how long it will take to accomplish something. If the task or activity is something you have not undertaken before, be rather generous when scheduling its completion.

From Priorities and Goals to Daily Activities

"I'm committed to my priorities and goals, but how do I coordinate these with my daily routine? I've got deadlines, you know!" I know. You *can* align your daily responsibilities, activities, and interests in accordance with your chosen priorities and goals. Read on.

Accumulations cost you double—you don't take action on them and you keep confronting them. To handle the array of items competing for your attention, and to balance big goals with the daily grind, collect everything on your desk and elsewhere that may need attention.

Operation Clean Sweep

Have you collected *everything?* Good. Stack it all up in front of you in a temporary pile. I don't care how high it gets; in fact, the higher the better—you'll have a much clearer idea of what you've allowed to accumulate and what you're up against.

Within a span of thirty minutes or less, you're going to rip through this collection of breathing space–threatening items.

Ready?

Without sentiment or hesitation, allocate each item to one of four locations—an Important pile, an Urgent pile, an Interesting pile, or the recycling bin (waste basket). Caution: Do *not* attempt this when you are tired or otherwise not fully alert because this process will seem overwhelming.

If an item is urgent *and* important place it in Important near the top. It it's simply urgent, place it in the appropriate pile.

If you are unsure of any particular item, you may place it at the bottom of the large stack, but only once for each item. On the second encounter, you have to classify it.

Within thirty minutes, the mess is gone.

Operation Clean Sweep has left you with three semineat piles. Rank the items and then rearrange them in each pile. Downgrade or toss anything you can. You're left with three smaller, more precisely arranged piles, Important (in accordance with your priorities and professional responsibilities), Urgent, and Interesting.

Starting with the Important pile, estimate how long it will take to complete each item. Add all your estimates and multiply that number by 1.5. Do the same with the other piles.

As the number of task hours before you climbs into the hundreds, as it may, you can see dramatically that there is no point continuing as you have. Your solution will vary based on the nature of your work, the available resources (such as helpers), and other particulars of the situation.

What does not vary is the ever-present opportunity before you to get meaner and leaner, and more focused. What else can you chuck? What can be combined/ignored/delayed/delegated/done in multiples/farmed out/automated/systemized, etc.? The more items you can downgrade to Interesting, the further ahead you'll be. Interesting can be relocated away from your desk.

For those items that can be handled another day, simply slip them into a daily or monthly tickler file. If the materials are too big to go into the tickler file, put a project note in the file, and neatly house the materials in another location, but away from your desk and not in sight.

As each new day or period of high anxiety over all the tasks you face ensues, repeat Operation Clean Sweep and remember to include the items in that day's tickler file.

I've used this procedure for eleven years, though

I only named it following the Persian Gulf war. After trying dozens of others—software systems, to-do lists, and other job scheduling and project logging systems—I've found that nothing else will get you moving as fast and as focused as Operation Clean Sweep.

This procedure can be used in tandem with what you already use, such as a to-do list, because you may have a need to look at the roster of tasks facing you with one glance. However, Operation Clean Sweep is so immediate and so responsive to the tasks you face, especially for shorter-duration tasks, you may find yourself abandoning the others. You'll also find yourself dropping nonimportant, nonurgent tasks.

When you need a change of pace, flip to the Urgent pile. The Interesting pile can be reviewed intermittently, perhaps every couple of days or weeks. It's okay if it grows very thick. Eventually, you'll reclassify or chuck its contents.

Ultimately, there are only three things you can do with whatever is glutting your desk and office—act on it, file it, or toss it.

FRESH AIR: Whenever you find folders and tasks mounting up on all sides of you, remember how they got there, and that you are in charge of them, not vice versa.

After you've identified the most important project or task—the one at the top of the Important folder—begin working on it to its completion. If you can't complete it because it requires input from others or for some other reason, proceed with it as far as you can go. Then place it back in the folder, either on top or where you determine it now belongs.

As long as you work on one project at a time, you *can* handle anything. There's not a software program you can't master, for example, as long as you work exclusively on learning the instructions. Moreover, no other approach to tasks will work faster.

In a like manner, begin on the next most important project and proceed as far as you can go. All the while, your priorities and goals are your guideposts.

The Big Drop

Let me say this as gently as I can—in this society, in this era, recognize that most items will have to be dropped. There will always be far more items competing for attention than you can manage comfortably. To keep your priorities, goals, and daily activities aligned, clear out what doesn't belong.

Dropping is not easy. Old habits, the familiar, what once mattered—all are difficult to give up.

Here is how to drop activities:

❏ Review your priorities list, then, for each item you face, ask, "Does this support my priorities?"
❏ Temporarily drop something and see if you miss it. Often you will not.

❏ Ease it out; drop a little of it periodically.

❏ Ask others whether it's something you need to, want to, or have to keep doing. The feedback may surprise you.

❏ Go cold turkey (only for the brave!): "XYZ is out of my life." This is not as harsh as it sounds, since the decision usually follows sound reasoning.

THE *GOLDEN DROP* RULE

The more items of momentary interest that you can drop or ignore, the greater the chance of alignment, and the more breathing space in your life. Promise!

Getting Organized Now and for the Future

▬

Action springs not from thought, but
from a readiness for responsibility.
—DIETRICH BONHOEFFER, PHILOSOPHER

▬

Derek Bok, former president of Harvard University, achieved at least fifteen minutes of fame by saying, "If you think education is costly, try ignorance."

If you think getting organized is time-consuming, try disorganization. Who is likely to be most unorganized—those who haven't identified their priorities, or don't have a method for handling new information and new items?

On any given day, you may be able to engage successfully in Operation Clean Sweep, but week after week and month after month, how do you win the organization war? Let's start with some "knowns."

In light of the mega-realities, two things are likely: (1) remaining organized is a growing problem for you, and (2) you are probably retaining too many information items—you have overcollected and overfiled.

Much of what you have collected does not serve you or support your priorities and goals. Why do you overcollect? Because the overglut is endless, or because you can delay decision-making by procrastinating ("Instead of taking action, I'll simply save it"). Some people overcollect as a hedge against an uncertain future.

Becoming and staying organized takes effort and thought, while saving time and offering peace of mind. The not-so-great paradox is that you expend time to save time. If it's helpful, think of getting organized as preparation "to respond to life."

Tired of living in clutter, Sue reorganized her apartment. She cleared 20% of her drawers, closets, and files, tossing the old, making space for the new. And she feels great about it.

Breaking the Organizing Barrier

"Organizing is not a moral issue," says organization consultant Barbara Hemphill, author of *Taming the Paper Tiger*. "It is not neatness, it is effectiveness. It is not efficiency, it is a tool." To be organized is an individually experienced state of being.

"Organization exists in many forms," she says. "A desk or office that would drive you batty may be well organized for a coworker." Not everything needs to be "in its place"—as long as you know where items are and can access them freely.

Hemphill offers some basic organizing principles:

1. If you don't know what you have and you can't find it, it is of no use to you.
2. Just because it is interesting or expensive doesn't mean you have to keep it.
3. Being neat and being organized are not the same thing.

When you attempt to get organized, do you quit after a while, believing it's hopeless? No one is born with organizing skills; they are acquired along the way. The key to getting and staying organized is making the effort. For many it is a welcome relief to learn how long it will take—the equivalent of a full weekend and several week nights.

Q: Why do some people shun getting organized?

A: For whatever reason, they approach it with fear and trepidation. Like primitives who fear that a photograph of them captures their soul, some people think getting organized will somehow strip them of their inner essence. They become anxious about doing nothing but getting organized. Yet, getting organized is an essential element to more breathing space.

Seven Excuses for Not Getting Organized

Even when you know it makes sense to "clean house," many traps to getting started may await. Here are seven major excuses for failing to get started:

1. **"I have been meaning to."** If this is a familiar self-lament, then make getting personally and completely organized a high-ranking item in your life.
2. **"I have never been good at organizing . . ."** This is of no consequence. All is forgiven. The difference between people "who are good at organizing" and "not good" is that people who are organized recognize the effort required to maintain the organization. Those "not good" at organizing believe that somehow things "just get out of order" or "get lost." Some go so far as to think there are forces (other than the mega-realities!) operating in opposition to them.
3. **"I don't know how to get started."** Keep reading.
4. **"I have so many other things to do."** Of course you do; you will for the rest of your life. After getting organized, however, the other things "you have to do" will more directly support your priorities and goals, and you will have a clearer mental connection that they do.
5. **"Organizing will take too much time."** Initially, it takes one weekend and several week

nights. Keep considering what disorganization has cost you.

6. **"I don't see any value in organizing."** Many aspects of your life already are organized. Now you are about to extend the procedures to enhance personal control, which has great value.

7. **"It makes me anxious; I don't feel that I am accomplishing that much."** If you only toss unnecessary files and papers, creating more space, you will be accomplishing a great deal.

Milt H. knew that he needed to get organized, letting years pass without getting started. He would do anything but straighten out his files. Yet he spent untold hours looking for items, and was never in control. His nickname became "Lose It Milt," because he could not be trusted to return anything. This reputation hampered his career and working relationships.

Knowing where item are, such as necessary papers, backup supplies, and important phone numbers and addresses, puts you in charge of your life, and provides freedom to concentrate on creative, fulfilling work and not the clutter that surrounds you.

How Organized Are You?

Here is a short quiz. If you answer yes to any of

the following, the next few chapters will be of importance to you.

1. Do you spend five minutes or more looking for a letter or document? Forty-five to 75 seconds is all it needs to take. More than that and you're wasting everyone's time.
2. Are week-old papers on your desk? A desk is *not* a filing cabinet.
3. Do you have trouble finding a particular item in your desk that you use frequently? Maybe it's best left *on* your desk.
4. Do you believe you need to see everything in order to easily retrieve it? I.e., "If I can't see it, I don't trust myself to find where I've stored it." Overreliance on having to see "it" is an open prescription for a life of immense clutter and inefficiency.
5. Do you feel that you could be organized if you only had more space? More space is seldom the answer; filing or getting rid of what isn't important is.
6. Do you have piles of newspapers and magazines you haven't gotten around to reading? If you're thinking of reading these issues cover to cover, good luck.
7. Did you ever find something at the bottom of a pile that you didn't know was there? You're liable to lose anything! Break up your piles now.

The High Art of Filing

Today you must be at the right place
before the right time.
—ROSABETH MOSS KANTER,
PRESIDENT, GOODMEASURE

Being organized enables you to approach life efficiently. Yet practically speaking, much of getting
organized comes down to how you file, an unglamo-
rous tool for getting and staying organized. Filing
involves allocating printed information and materials into their best home, *for now*.

What do you need to be a good filer? Clear
priorities and goals, and the space to put a chair in
front of a filing cabinet. If you fear that filing means
you're becoming a caretaker, ask yourself what are
you becoming a caretaker of—that which *you* deem
important. If it isn't important, don't save it. If it is
important, why are you moaning about filing it?

Managing the Beforehand

A crucial step in organizing and filing effectively, in light of the mega-realities, is to condition your environments—your office, home, car, and other physical spaces of your life. This means that you arrange, stock, and maintain such spaces in a manner that supports your efforts.

Let's look at filing by introducing an important concept of breathing space—managing the "beforehand." Stanley M. Davis uses this term in *Future Perfect*. To condition your environments in accordance with what you face today is to accommodate inefficiency; you are merely managing the aftermath of intake overglut.

Managing the beforehand, as opposed to the aftermath, involves creating space—mentally or physically—in advance of what comes next. I regard it as clearing out the old and unsupportive, and making room for where you are heading, the new and supportive. It requires anticipation and vision.

Managing the beforehand helps integrate your priorities and goals with your personal "systems," including how to keep your desk, office, closets, car, and other spaces.

When managing the beforehand, you are perpetually turning over files and data. You know that more is coming which will supersede what you're holding, that your interests will change, and that it's psychologically costly to hold on to what you don't use.

The Joy of Sex

Your goal is to align the files and spaces in your life to accommodate where you want or need to devote your attention. Sorry, sex has nothing to do with this section. However, managing the beforehand is joyously simple. *You start by simply creating new files, independent of whether or not you have anything to put in them.* In other words, allocate space in advance for what you will be managing and collecting.

Quite magically, these files begin to fill. Managing the beforehand files requires anticipation. You may start a file only to end up tossing it. That's okay. Far better to have a few misses than attempt to support your priorities and goals without creating the space they will consume.

Few Things Are That Sacred. The process is dynamic—files come and files go, just like information comes and is replaced. The most accomplished among us do not let buildups occur.

Baby teeth, snakeskin, old appliances, and elected officials all get replaced. So does what you're holding on to so tightly. Continue to be gentle with yourself. It's not easy to know where to put every damned thing that crosses your desk.

Q: What are the file headings used for managing the beforehand?

A: They're personal. However, in reviewing your priorities and goals, many file headings become apparent. For example: * Letters and Correspondence * Monthly Bills * XYZ Bank * Warranties * Business Cards * Insurance * Mortgage * Properties * Johnny's Artwork * Discount Coupons to Restaurants * Certificates, Diplomas, and so on.

If you seek world travel in the future, then, logically, "World Travel" becomes a file heading. Other file labels might include "Investments," "Fitness and Longevity," "New Equipment," "Forthcoming Opportunities," or "Refresher Courses."

To accommodate the information overglut that you know is coming, you can start a file called "Review in One Month," "Hold for Clarity," or "Temporary Hold." The variations are many. Choose what suits you and continue to manage the beforehand. Allow for what you know or suspect is coming, so when it does, you're in control.

A word of caution. Files marked "Temporary Hold" or "Review in a Month" quickly grow large. That's fine. Simply getting them out of the way and keeping your desk clear enhances your sense of breathing space. Later, review these temporary files, and if you recognize that items belong elsewhere, put them in an appropriate file or chuck them. As always, the more you chuck from the start, the less glutted you remain.

These holding files take the place of what is often inconveniently strewn about your office or home: "I don't know what to do with this, so I'll just park it here (. . . and hope the organizing fairy comes by and does something with it)."

Holding files represent what you *may* give attention to in the future when you are prepared to do so.

Q: This is a little exciting. Do you mean to say that I can create a file for anything that I even think will be of importance?

A: Yes.

Q: But couldn't this contribute to overglut?

A: It could, except these new files are subject to the same rules as are all files—keep reevaluating what you retain and why. Often the files need to be merged or relabeled, or portions are best tossed or reassigned. It is a *dynamic* process.

Q: Then the ability to effectively file is an important skill for managing one's affairs, gaining space, and helping to prepare for future activities?

A: Yes. All true. Filing by managing the before-hand techniques is a tool that enhances your sense of breathing space.

FRESH AIR: If the prospect of tackling a whole file cabinet or all of your desk drawers at once leaves you gasping, break down the task by organizing the first half of the first drawer this week. In subsequent weeks, tackle the other portions. Shortly, the job will be done, and you will feel good about the process and yourself.

PART

III

POWER TOOLS

Conditioning Your Work Environment

Do what you can, with what you have,
where you are.
—THEODORE ROOSEVELT, 26TH
PRESIDENT OF THE UNITED STATES

Conditioning your work environment, coordinating the arrangement of physical spaces in your life in an anticipatory, supportive manner, works well for far more than your files. You can apply the principles to your entire office (and your home and car; see next chapter).

No matter whether yours is a corporate or home office—let's see how to gain more breathing space. Obviously, you will have more leeway if you are self-employed, or the "boss," but the principles work much the same.

First a truism: Life is a desk. To prehistoric man, life was a spear. To the frontiersman, life was a rifle. Today, life is a desk.

In the over-information era, your desk has to be a comfortable place for you. What does it say if your desk is a continuing mess? You met the din, and the din won.

The quality and ambience of your work space works best when it demonstrates *the quality and ambience of your life,* or how you would like your life to be. What do you want and need *on* your desk, *in* it, and *near* it? It varies for each of us.

Suggestions for the top of your desk:

❑ Computer equipment
❑ Clear, open space
❑ Telephone or communication device
❑ Frequently used items

Periodically assess different items that support your desktop arrangement, such as computer trays, hanging lamps, and swivel mechanisms to conveniently move equipment as needed.

One of the benefits of product overload is that you can find exactly the item you need or want to make you feel more comfortable and be more productive at your desk. Whatever the item, as you begin reaping the benefits, you will quickly forget the cost. Would you give up your fax machine if you could get the money back?

To create more surface space, you could use a mechanical arm that hoists your PC monitor over the desk. It swings forward and back, and left and right. I have one and don't know how I lived without it.

FRESH AIR: Joe Sugarman, in his book, *Success Forces*, explains that by clearing your desk every evening, you automatically have to *choose* what to work on the next day. Though such reasoning is contrary to the advice of "time management" experts, I wholeheartedly endorse it.

Clearing your desk each evening reduces having to conduct Operation Clean Sweep. It is a discipline that yields a marvelous sense of breathing space with which to start each day.

Every evening after you've cleared your desk, acknowledge yourself for what you accomplished that day. Don't beat yourself up for what you didn't do. You're doing the best you can. If you can do better, you will, maybe not at once, but soon enough.

Use the end of the day, slow periods, or periods of low personal energy to revamp your files, keep your desk orderly, and better prepare yourself for high-octane output when you're ready to get started again.

What else do you need? I keep a pitcher of water nearby. For me, dehydration, more than anything else, is the major reason for low productivity. In half of the cases when you think you're tired, you're really only thirsty.

To create my own workout, I keep some items on the far end of my desk so that I have to reach to use them.

FRESH AIR: You may need two desks. "Two desks?" I am not suggesting that the solution to more breathing space is more filing and desk space. Indeed, as more time is not the answer to alleviating time pressure, more space is seldom the answer to being better organized. You may need the second desk, or other clear surface area to do creative work, if your present desk is primarily an administrative outpost.

Administrative outposts are useful and necessary for coexisting with the din. Yet, often they are not conducive to ground-breaking tasks, original thinking, or emergency projects.

What About Inside Your Desk? Include frequently needed supplies, but remember: A desk is not a supply cabinet. Maintain a drawer of personal items—your desk is there to support you. Tissues and Velamints are okay.

Include any needed forms or heavily used items, but leave a 20 percent vacancy. To manage the beforehand means reserving space for what's coming. Constantly review what you're holding and decide to retain or toss it.

Near Your Desk. Near but not on goes the loving and familiar—pictures, plants, and motivators. Also install any supporting accoutrements, from Vita-Lites to ocean wave music, if they support your productivity, efficiency, and creativity.

If Moses went to the top of Mount Sinai today, here's what he might bring down to us:

THE TEN COMMANDMENTS OF DESKMANSHIP

---

1. Thou shalt clear thy desk every night. Yes, every night.
2. Thou shalt continually refine what goes on thy desktop.
3. Thou shalt not use thy desktop as a filing cabinet.
4. Thou shalt predetermine what belongs inside thy desk.
5. Thou shalt keep 20 percent of the drawer space vacant.
6. Thou shalt furnish thy surrounding office to support thy desk.
7. Thou shalt take comfort when at thy desk.
8. Thou shalt keep clean thy desk and thy surrounding area.
9. Thou shalt leave thy desk periodically.
10. Thou shalt honor thy desk as thyself.

"Thou shalt continually refine what goes on thy desktop" implies that what you used to keep on your desk because it was convenient and useful may no longer be so.

"Thou shalt keep clean thy desk and thy surrounding area" is important for maintaining control. "Thou shalt take comfort when at thy desk" means that your desk needs to be a comfortable place for you, not a war zone.

Reflecting on the ninth commandment, "leave thy desk," I find that a good workout the night before helps me to view my desk as a friendly place. When you've exercised long and hard, sitting at your desk is like a vacation.

"Conditioning" Investments

To ensure that your desk and office environment supports you, *invest in yourself.* If you need them, room dividers and sound barriers are available in a wide variety of shapes and sizes and can improve upon any existing sound barriers.

The gentle, rhythmic "white noise" of a small fan's motor serves as a sound buffer to many of the sounds that may distract you. Maybe you want a couch for quick catnaps during the day.

When It Comes to Technology, Buy! My friend Bob won't spend $100 for a pocket dictator to save six hours a week. "The firm ought to pay for it. Why should I spend my money on it?" he simpers.

Phil, self-employed, won't spend $500 to double his hard disk storage capacity. So he shuffles floppy disks all day and loses productivity.

Whether or not your organization will pick up the tab, what is it, right now, that you know will increase your efficiency? A modem? A pocket dictator? A desktop copier? A laser printer?

Rule of thumb: Any item that saves you one hour per week for a minimum of one year and costs $1,000 or less is an excellent buy.

Rule of forefinger: Never mind if you purchased the latest or fastest model; there will *always* be later and faster models.

Conditioning Your Other Environments

If I had eight hours to chop down a tree, I'd spend six hours sharpening my ax.

—ABRAHAM LINCOLN

Your home is your castle unless you fall into the moat and are eaten by crocodiles. To ensure that your home environment enhances your sense of breathing space, don't allow ad hoc outposts to build up: Take the utility bills *out* of the punch bowl on the dining room table.

Adopt effective docking and unloading techniques. Always bring mail, office work brought home, tax receipts, and items purchased, including warranties and tags, to their final destinations or to your administrative outpost for processing and integration into your organization system.

The more you are able to keep flat surfaces

clear—the dining room table, your desk, small tables—the greater your ability to manage the flow of items in your life, deal with them capably, and move on. You experience a wonderful sense of breathing space.

Q: So conditioning my environment requires forethought, but remaining organized starts when I come in the door?

A: Yes. Avoid leaving things at *inappropriate* outposts. If an item belongs in the den, take it to the den. If it belongs in the closet, go to the closet.

When you fail to take items to their end destinations, you create double and triple work for yourself. And you feel overwhelmed. Upon returning from travel, immediately unpack your bags, put clothes in the closet or washer, and take all paperwork to your desk.

The Home Phone. "Good evening, Mr. Davidson, how are you this evening?" "Fine, and I don't want to buy, contribute to, invest in, or receive anything, thank you."

As solicitations to home phones increase, so does the total of unlisted numbers. More than 30 percent of U.S. home telephone numbers are unlisted. Its drawbacks are apparent, but depending on how much you want to protect your castle, you might consider it.

FRESH AIR: If you keep a phone by your bed, you're asking for punishment.

Using the Multiple-Stations Technique

If you wear contact lenses, you already know the value of using multiple stations. You lens wearers know to keep extra saline solution and storage tubes at the various stations of your life: your desk, car, locker at the gym, etc. Hence, you are always prepared without having to carry these materials.

What else can be stored at multiple stations, freeing you of having to carry it or be concerned with it? Pens, note pads, calendars? It's your choice. What else is inexpensive, often used, and easily missed, such as a comb or brush, umbrella, or even the kids' medicine?

Here are two guiding principles to using multiple stations:

Anything temporarily housed in the wrong location adds to clutter and consumes your time.

Conversely, anything you *need* at various checkpoints in your life is best stored there.

Your Home "Out-basket"

If you keep a small cabinet or table by the door, use it only for what is leaving your home, *never* for what is entering. What enters goes directly to its final resting place; what exits departs soon. The process is continual.

FRESH AIR: If mornings are a super rush for you, lighten your load first by reducing the number of items you have to round up and things you have to do. Visit your car the *night before*. Stock it with whatever you or your crew needs for the next day. This includes office folders, books, gym clothes, lunch bags—anything that won't spoil.

Conditioning Your Car

Keep a roll of dimes and quarters stored unobtrusively in your car, along with a copy of all important phone numbers, a pad, pen, stamps, and envelopes.

Also maintain an extra, concealed wallet with credit cards and library cards; a gym bag with socks, underwear, and a toothbrush; sunglasses, tissues, flashlight, maps of the area, and a container of gas additive, in addition to car registration, a first aid kit, jumper cables, tools, and other safety devices.

Install a cassette deck or compact disc player in your car, a key item for conditioning your environment. When stuck in traffic, Mozart, a tape review of your meeting, or a motivational cassette all help. Also keep a book in your car.

I have all these in my car stored in small gym bags and an old briefcase. I keep backup car keys in my house and backup house keys hidden in my car. I have extra car keys in a faithful "Hide-a-Key" compartment that attaches magnetically under the bumper. *You'll* never find it.

I keep photocopied pages of all my cards and credit cards in my briefcase and in a file at home labeled "Cards and Credit Cards." I have a map indicating the location of all the libraries in my area.

When you are acutely aware of the cost of being locked out of your car, delayed, or stuck in the city unprepared, you'll get prepared.

Q: The key, then, to maintaining a conditioned environment is to handle items as they accumulate?

A: Yes. Use a "pay as you go" system—no piles, no ad hoc outposts, no accumulations. You will be astounded by your enhanced sense of breathing space.

FRESH AIR: Once you develop the habit of clearing space, and I mean in *all the compartments of your life:* your car, your closets, medicine cabinets, etc., you accomplish many things. You demonstrate to yourself that you do indeed have enough space to manage your affairs and conduct your life; and you keep in a ready state to handle what is next rather than trying to get by.

Controlling Intake Overglut

The art of being wise is the art of
knowing what to overlook.
—WILLIAM JAMES, PIONEER IN
PSYCHOLOGY

The human tongue, science tells us, contains
about 9,000 taste buds. The human nose, with learning, can discern more than 7,500 fragrances. The
human eye, with training, can detect a combined
total of more than 10,000 shades and hues of 150
basic colors. Thank God, we have these wondrous
sensory ranges. Thank God, we don't have to use
them all.

On that sweet morning when you've gotten your
life in order, the over-information era and its inces-
sant rancor will continue to flood your senses, with
more coming in by afternoon. Like the alien in *Alien,*

it just keeps attacking. Unlike Sigourney Weaver, you can't kill it. The overglut is endless.

Suppose you've whipped everything into shape. A critical aspect to maintaining breathing space is preventing the overglut from creeping back in, as best you can. Four of the biggest culprits are:

❑ Junk mail;
❑ Mismanaged reading;
❑ Other people's clutter; and
❑ Packratism (as in packrat, not Pacman).

We'll tackle the first three in this chapter, saving packratism for the next.

Eliminating Junk Mail

Traditionally, books on time management discuss how often to handle a piece of paper. Some say once. Some say twice. It always depends on what the paper says.

FRESH AIR: The ideal number of times to handle most pieces of paper is zero, by not receiving them in the first place!

When you make a purchase by mail, your name is sold and circulated to dozens of catalog houses. Even your state's Department of Motor Vehicles sells its list of licensed drivers to anyone with money. The nerve.

In an era in which each piece of mail adds to environmental glut, it's a civic duty, as well as an effective technique for achieving breathing space, to reduce the amount of junk mail you receive. You can eliminate 40 percent of your junk mail with *one* letter. Write to:

Mail Preference Service
Direct Marketing Association
11 West 42nd Street
P.O. Box 3861
New York, NY 10163-3861

Tell them: "I would like my name removed from your direct mail lists." Sending this letter will effectively reduce your junk mail for three to six months. Thereafter, keep sending them the same letter.

To trace who is selling your name when you make a mail order purchase or a donation, add a code to the end of your street address such as "1A" or "2D." Later, if you receive mail with your coded address, you know who sold your name to whom.

When making any mail order purchase, feel free to mention or include a preprinted label that reads:

IMPORTANT NOTICE: I DON'T WANT MY NAME PLACED ON ANY MAILING LISTS WHATSOEVER, AND FORBID THE USE, SALE, RENTAL, OR TRANSFER OF MY NAME.

You also can fight junk mail by saving all of it for weeks. Then hire a high school student at $4.50 per hour to send a form letter to every party who has sent to you more than once. Explain carefully and cordially that you have no interest in their offer. Resist the Promethean urge to fight the overglut by yourself. As we'll describe shortly, you can employ students part-time for many tasks.

Managing Your Reading

The typical career professional faces one to four hours a day of job-related reading. Executive or homemaker, managing your reading will enhance your sense of breathing space.

Read periodicals and books at a table. Get paper, scissors, postage, and file folders ready. If you encounter something you choose to enter into your system, you can do so easily.

If you're merely pleasure-reading, relax—the following is not applicable. While it may seem ruthless at first, tear out or copy only those pages of magazines, newsletters, and reports that currently appear important to you. Copy key pages from books. Get to the essence, which is all you can ingest and act upon anyway.

FRESH AIR: Professional subscriptions, the very publications we *asked* to receive, are part of the overglut. Most of the publications you receive, clearly, are worth the money. The question to keep asking yourself, given the reality of the clutter and information overglut, is "Are they worth my time?" *Try reading every second or third issue. You'll find you won't miss much.*

For quick relief, call the subscription offices of the publications you receive—they all have toll-free 800 numbers. Ask to have your subscriptions discontinued and to receive any refunds to which you're entitled.

The sheer joy and guilt-free feeling of not having to read publications because you've paid for them make canceling them more than worth the effort. Alternatively, if you receive several of the same type of magazine, pick the one publication that serves more of your needs.

Help Me Make It Through the Pile. Practice skimming, reading the first sentence of each paragraph, and scanning, looking through the entire body of your material to see which parts are important to you.

Delegate quantities of reading material to your part-timers or staff at work. It won't take you but ten minutes of instruction and a few follow-up sessions to train others to quickly find and highlight topics of interest to you.

While helpful to some people, speed-reading courses may not be your answer. Like speed-listening, it's not clear what the downside effect is on your well-being. We use our senses at certain "speeds." As humankind evolves, we may be able to comfortably intake data faster. For now, the jury is still out.

Read When You're In. Most people attempt to handle reading chores when they go out of town, believing that this is a good method of "catching up." When you read while out of town, however, what happens?

While traveling, you don't have your copier, scissors, envelopes, and files—items to help you *act* upon what you've read. And you may not have the desire or energy to follow through when you return. Cut down your reading on business travel.

Conversely, many people don't want to write when traveling, and feel that writing is something they must do back home or at the office. In terms of efficiency and breathing space, just the opposite is true.

FRESH AIR: Reading is best handled at a fixed address. Writing, especially with the advent of laptops, pocket dictators, and other portable goodies, can be handled ably in the relative seclusion of a plane seat or hotel. You usually can't write when you are "in" anyway; there are too many distractions!

And now a word about the Sunday paper. "You're not suggesting I give that up?!" Maybe. Do you devoutly read the Sunday newspaper? If it's a pleasurable activity that you enjoy, keep doing it. If you are reading the paper believing that you need to (or can!) keep up, or it is the thing to do, STOP. Only buy a copy when you *choose* to read it.

When you read about a government official who has committed improprieties, you consume part of your day. What is the long-term benefit to you of such reading?

Dealing with Other People's Clutter

You sense it immediately: Visiting someone else's office, you see reports and folders piled high and a desktop strewn with papers. Things are in disarray. You know that you have little chance of being treated efficiently by this person.

You don't have the resources to straighten him out. Sometimes, of course, you have no choice but to deal with this person. Heavens above, he or she may be your boss, or your spouse!

Aaron is a staff writer for a local magazine. His job involves reporting to an editor who is hopelessly deluged with clutter. Aaron knows that the editor's job involves handling an endless stream of paperwork. This editor's office and desk, however, have many more stacks and piles than Aaron has ever seen in one room.

Aaron's solution is ensuring that his submitted work will be easily found by buying 100 fire-engine-red report folders and always turning in his clearly labeled assignments in these folders.

When you have the option, avoid dealing with clutter bugs—a decision you'll have to face with increasing frequency as the five mega-realities overcome more people.

16

Combating Packratism: Stripping Your Files

> If you're not changing constantly, you're probably not going to be accommodating the reality of your world.
>
> —WILLIAM G. MCGOWAN, FOUNDER AND CHAIRMAN, MCI, INC.

In a society that speeds off in all directions, it's understandable that you'd like to hang on to *pieces of the past*. Packratism, now epidemic in America, is not the answer. Careful consideration is in order.

In combating packratism, first remember: You remain the primary force preventing the overglut from engulfing you. To take control, eliminate, at the top, whatever clogs your system and interferes with your effectiveness.

We all tend to overcollect. Organizational consultants are fond of saying that clutter is a sign of postponed decision-making, but this is far too simplistic an explanation. It can also be a sign of play-ing the victim, having no focus, or finding comfort in materialism.

When it comes to paper, you probably need to toss most of what's in your files, but we'll go easy for now. The three principles of combating packrat-ism are to (1) break down horizontal piles, (2) reread your priority list and ask key questions, (3) master the art of creative trashing.

1. *Break down horizontal piles.* You cannot man-age a horizontal pile; indeed, no one can efficiently negotiate this spatial arrangement. During Opera-tion Clean Sweep, you get to stack up one major horizontal pile, but only for a matter of minutes.

> Human beings most effectively organize printed information vertically, either in a fil-ing cabinet with all labeled tabs facing up-ward, or in a vertical divider with tabs facing outward.

Horizontal piles cannot be a final resting place for the items in them because you also have to do something else with them. To know in seconds whether or not someone is efficient, visit his office or home and observe whether he maintains horizon-tal piles.

2. *Reread your list of priorities and goals.* Then wade through each of your files and ask yourself four questions:

❑ Have I used this information in the last year?
❑ Are there any consequences of not retaining it?

❏ Does it support me, my family, job, community, etc.?

❏ Is the information/item irreplaceable?

Feel free to retain the item(s) if you answer *yes* to any of the above questions. Nevertheless, in light of what you now know, your priorities, and the surrounding overglut, is retention warranted? So often the answer is "Toss it."

In my speeches, I sometimes say to audiences: "In the immortal words of Edwin Bliss, 'When in doubt . . .'" Then I pause and let them finish. In one group, however, a man in the middle row called out, ". . . whip it out."

Okaaaaay . . . end of audience participation.

The phrase concludes with ". . . throw it out."

3. *Master the art of creative trashing.* What else can you toss right now that otherwise barely exceeds the criteria for retention?

❏ Which books can you give away? What information that is old hat to you would be welcome to a newer member of your organization?

❏ How many bags and boxes of old clothes and books can you donate to the Salvation Army or Goodwill? What about the hospitals, schools, libraries, and retirement homes in your area? It's a lot easier to let go of items when you know they will benefit others.

❏ Place a box where you can see it in a closet, pantry, or other area and add to it as you discover clothes that don't fit or items you choose not to hold on to.

❑ When the bag or box is full, drop it off. In addition to reducing the clutter in your home, you have now contributed to a worthy cause.

Consider every piece of paper, junk mail solicitation, document, book, article of clothing, anything you retain that does not support your priorities, as hazardous to your breathing space and best tossed while still fresh. **Declare your freedom from the clutter syndrome, which is endemic to twentieth-century man and woman.**

Once you adopt intake overglut control measures, maintenance gets easier and easier.

❑ At least quarterly, reexamine *everything* you own and practice creative trashing. This will get easier and go faster each time you do it.

❑ Prune your holdings one week before your birthday, and near New Year's Day. The realization of years passing just before your birthday or other notable milestone prompts you to toss what does not support you.

❑ If you have to, allow yourself one file drawer, closet, or storage locker as a dumping ground for whatever mess you want to accumulate. If you don't get rid of that stuff eventually, however, your executors will, and they'll charge your heirs for doing it!

Normally, this chapter ends with the sentence above. However, because you're a special case and are still reluctant to part with much of your vast holdings, this copy of **Breathing Space** includes a couple of extra pages.

Overcoming Second Thoughts on Tossing

You know you are retaining too much but reflexively you seek to hang on:

Q: What if I need this later? Shouldn't I hold on to it just in case?

A. How long will you hang on to white elephants, information crutches, and yesterday's news? When will you start trusting yourself? To overcome second thoughts on tossing, make function follow form. The guiding principle is: You only have so much space, and thank goodness it's not more!

Pretend you only had a two-foot cube to pack all data items of importance in your life. Could you do it? For nearly everyone, the answer is a resounding YES.

If you're still in a quandary about tossing things, try this approach: View the item(s) or information on five consecutive days. If the item is best retained or is of value, then you intuitively feel this during each review. At any point, you may toss the item. After the five reviews, feel free to retain it.

When you want to toss something, but are getting weak in the knees, as reinforcement, recall how good it felt to toss other items, how months passed and how you never missed them. Then remember that in the over-information era, injudicious attachment to information and things becomes the greatest impediment to breathing space. The ability to let them go is heaven.

A Blast From the Past. As further reinforcement against over-collecting in the present, look to your past. Review old tax returns or checkbooks and reexamine all of your prior purchases, deductions, and check stubs. If you saved credit card receipts or phone bills, scan them.

You may be struck by the incongruity between your chosen priorities and what you have been paying for and accumulating.

P.S.—Every year, your tax receipts from three years earlier can be tossed safely because the government will no longer come after you for those years (unless it's a criminal suit!). So save copies of the forms you filed. The rest can go. . . .

Oh, It's No Use! If you can't bear to part with what you've collected, may God bless you. Here are some parting options:

❏ Set up your own "informational retrieval plan." Copy the title pages, cover pages, mastheads, addresses, and/or phone numbers onto single pages, add them to data base software programs, or scan them.

❏ Develop a single file or three-ring notebook, labeled "Just in Case," specifically for these one-page files. Now you can find references quickly if you need to while not being bogged down.

❏ Box and store items of "possible future use."

Remove them from your office, home, or immediate work area. Mark the box: "Review contents in April."

Whenever you want, feel free to box and store items "of possible future use." Mark your calendar for a six- or twelve-month review, but get the box out of your office or home.

You are the primary and
indeed only force that
can prevent the overglut
from engulfing you.

PART
IV

CEREBRAL TOOLS

17

Completions: The End of Racing the Clock

A thousand years in thy sight are but
as yesterday when it is past, and as a
watch in the night.
—94TH PSALM

A powerful way to gain breathing space, perpetually, is by seeking completions, a notion championed by Robert Fritz in his ground-breaking book, *The Path of Least Resistance.* You are already a master of many aspects of completion.

When you awake each morning, you have completed sleep for that night. When you know you are ready to turn in a big report at work, that is a completion. If you were to get nothing else from this book but guidance on using completions, then you would have benefited greatly.

Large or small, completions provide a mental and emotional break. They make you feel good.

139

Simply putting away the dishes, or taking out the garbage, is a completion that yields benefits. You can continually gain completions in every area of your life. They can be achieved on multiyear projects, or activities that only last a few seconds.

Achieving completions is energizing because it offers a clean end to activities or even thoughts, and a good beginning for what's next.

The happiest, most productive, most prosperous people have developed the habit of achieving one completion after another, acknowledging themselves for their efforts, the experiences, and the accomplishments. Yet, to an observer, it may look as if there is barely a moment to catch a breath.

Those who have mastered completion often are able to quickly and effectively give silent self-acknowledgment and then move on: "I did a particularly good job on this and it's rewarding to have it done."

They are not obsessive and do not seek completions only for completion's sake. Indeed, achieving completions is not synonymous with obsessive behavior, clock-chasing, or overachieving. Completions are simply effective means for giving your mind and emotions temporary energy breaks.

Not Just for Monumental Efforts. Completions can be acknowledged when finishing a subtask. They are analogous to driving along a scenic mountain highway and stopping periodically at scenic overlooks to get a breath of fresh air, stretch out, acknowledge how far you have come and where you are.

Olivia was a health care consultant to several organizations. To complete each engagement, she had to prepare and deliver a final report. In years past, Olivia thought it enough to write, proof, and word-process the entire report for on-schedule delivery to the client.

Previously, Olivia would tie up loose ends several days or weeks *after* delivering the report, while in the midst of other activities.

Recognizing the power of completions, however, Olivia built binding the report, producing an attractive cover, and making an easy delivery into her schedule. She updated her hard-copy file, completed project logs, cost data, and invoices. She streamlined her working notes file. She even gave the client a phone call one day in advance to alert them that the report was coming.

By viewing all aspects of the engagement as a unit, Olivia was able to complete all related activities by the day the report was delivered.

Olivia was clear mentally and emotionally by the end of the day. She felt good about her accomplishment and was energized to start what came next, the following morning.

Encouraging Completions

Gaining completions is facilitated by literally creating space in advance of what you know is coming, and hence is supported by managing the beforehand techniques. This enables you to maintain control. You focus on what you choose, rather than being inundated by what confronts you.

Keeping your work space clear is a completion. Eliminating items from your daily activities list is a completion. Quickly scanning and assessing new intake, and tossing most of it, is a major completion!

Maintaining a "clean house" is the environment for completion. Make this fun. Make it automatic.

Protect Your Space. Measures that protect your breathing space are important. A variation on gaining completion is to not initiate activities you don't intend to support. How often do you incur paperwork or engage in activities because you do not say no?

FRESH AIR: Saying no to what doesn't interest you enables you to say yes more often and gain completion of what does interest you.

For some reason, we all tend to say yes when the request for our participation is off in the future. We fantasize that several weeks or months from now, we'll feel much less pressured than now. Often, as that future date arrives, we see our commitment as another intrusion. Protect your schedule for now and the future.

P.S.: When you say no to someone, couch it in positive terms, such as "Thanks, but not for me." Then, thank yourself for your new-found control.

Also, say no to the next TV show. Say no to getting dressed with the radio on. Say yes to visualizing how you'd like your day to go.

THE ESCALATION OF TIME-RELATED PHRASES

Do you tell others to "wait a second" when you mean a minute? To enhance your sense of breathing space, use such phrases more accurately, giving both you and the other party the chance for more completions:

PHRASE	ALL TOO COMMON MEANING
Wait a second	About 60 seconds.
Momentarily	About 60 seconds.
Shortly	1 to 3 minutes.
A couple of minutes	3 to 10 minutes.
A little while	8 to 15 minutes.
Not much longer	5 to 30 minutes.
An hour or so	2 to 4 hours.
A couple of hours	4 to 6 hours.
A couple of days	About a week.
A couple of weeks	About a month.
A couple of months	6 to 9 months.
Next year	Three years from now.

The Ill Effects of Incompletions

When you leave tasks or activities uncompleted, you have energy vested in them. To effectively engage in long-term projects, acknowledge your completions at various milestones. Divide and conquer.

Many people create a series of incompletions, professionally and personally, task-wise and psychologically. The unhappiest among us continually ponder what is incomplete instead of simply acknowledging the actual situation, and then making new choices about what action to take.

Lack of completions in relationships often blocks divorced individuals from meeting a new mate with whom they could have a happy, lasting relationship. Lack of completions at work leaves one feeling exhausted and used.

Frequently, people will tell me they want to leave for the day with everything done on the daily to-do list or in the "Important" folder.

Whether you checked off all you had listed is moot. It was arbitrary to begin with. You didn't know how long the tasks would actually take, or what unforeseen impediments might arise. Otherwise, you'd complete your objectives every day.

FRESH AIR: If you want to leave each night with everything "done," give yourself acknowledgment for completing what you did complete. Acknowledging yourself for what you did get done is the surest method of leaving without feeling beaten, and is usually uplifting.

Avoid the Post-vacation Slam

Your big vacation is ending. For seven days it was all blue sky and clear blue sea. You return home, and the first day back at work what happens? You have a stack of phone messages on your desk. Your mail is nine inches high. There are memos, reports, and messages all over your desk.

The benefits of your vacation are all but negated. The overglut rears its ugly head again. You've been slammed.

On that first day back, and often the second, you can experience extreme pressure to catch up. The same thing can happen when you are on an overnight trip or out of the office all day. The moment you return, the whole world falls in on you.

You can avoid this kind of pressure by applying completion thinking, supported by managing the beforehand techniques.

FRESH AIR: Plan your vacation so that you return one day before you told everybody you would. Include a decompression phase in your plans; your trip is not complete until you comfortably reintegrate yourself into your home and office.

You are far better off taking one less vacation day and building in a day for transition and decompression than coming back too abruptly. Avoid returning to the office on a Monday; Mondays are already high-pressured. Manage the beforehand so that when you return, you feel good about having been away, and you feel good about being back. Avoid pre-vacation anxiety as well by allocating only a modest amount to do the day before leaving.

Before you leave, instruct others to filter, reroute, or handle as many phone calls as possible; and, based on instructions, to segment your important, urgent, and interesting accumulations.

Return to a clean office, a clean desk, a clean home, and a clean car. Acknowledge yourself for having an enjoyable trip and for achieving this completion.

FRESH AIR: When you travel or, for that matter, take on any task, go beyond half-way before taking a "mid-way" pause. By taking care of the "heavy half" first, and acknowledging this completion, you are more energized to complete the shorter, lighter second half.

More Completions Every Day

The fastest way to begin achieving completions is to identify those you are already achieving—big or small. What are the completions during your typical day? At work? At home? In your life?

Deriving the greatest benefit from completions requires continually acknowledging yourself for them. For reinforcement, list your completions, large and small, from yesterday. . . .

1. _____
2. _____
3. _____

Now, cite three things to be completed currently. . . .

1. _____
2. _____
3. _____

Cite three more items that you can complete within a month.

1. _____
2. _____
3. _____

The Biggest Completion You've Ever Experienced

Nope, it's not getting married or getting that big raise or having your first child. The biggest completion of your life is occurring as you finish the next paragraph, as you realize that you've had the time and the space to handle *everything in your life so far that you have completed*. Oooh, that's heavy.

All the bad days and good days, small triumphs and large triumphs, rushed times and relaxed times that you've completed up to this moment, are, obviously, completed.

When you realize that all of your completions are history, *the present takes on a vibrance and energy* enabling you to achieve more and feel more at ease.

FRESH AIR: You are whole and complete right now. You can acknowledge the completion of your life thus far, each day.

Get about twelve hours of sleep this Saturday or Sunday, awake and acknowledge yourself for having a long, deep sleep, and you're as "caught up" as one can get.

FRESH AIR: One night each week, go to bed by 9 P.M. The next morning, you will feel like a million dollars, and be able to tackle anything. As often as possible, sleep before you are exhausted. You don't have to knock yourself out to earn the right to sleep.

Continue to use your daily retirement as a major completion: "I acknowledge myself for completing this day. This day is over. I am now ready for deep, restful sleep."

Creating Space

All happiness depends on a leisurely breakfast.

—JOHN GUNTHER, AUTHOR
AND CULTURAL HISTORIAN

Your company is sending you to a two-day conference. It will be held on a Saturday and Sunday, starting at 8 A.M. and ending at 5 P.M. The reservations have already been made.

You have scheduled the conference on your calendar and made all the necessary preparations. You are ready to go. Surprise! The conference is canceled. It is early morning of what would have been the first day. You now have gained two solid days.

Envision a fifteen-week course held each Wednesday evening from 7 to 10 P.M. You are registered to attend. It, too, gets canceled. You now have three hours each Wednesday evening to pursue what you believed you could not get to.

Caution: How will you fill the void? By exposing yourself to more overglut? Or can you opt to take a walk, review your photo album, or sketch? Will you learn a new language or visit friends?

What you do with this bonanza is up to you. This period is always available—not necessarily each day, but in the course of any stretch of days it is there for the taking.

FRESH AIR: If your calendar "tends" to fill up, to create space, cancel something already scheduled.

Periodically fill in your calendar with nonwork and nonproductive activities. These activities could include enjoying your family, having lunches and dinners, staying in shape, or simply taking a stroll.

You don't have to devote every moment to work or to productive activities. *Not taking a breather directly contributes to your lack of breathing space.*

More Ways for Creating Space

The Winning Minute. You say you don't have a moment to relax; every part of your day is taken? Linger an extra minute at lunch, in the men's/ladies' room, and at your desk at the start and close of each day. This allows you to have transitions between activities and decreases your feeling of being rushed.

Also, recall a pleasant experience or time when you felt particularly relaxed or calm. Just recalling pleasant experiences brings on the feeling of relaxation.

Help Is a Phone Call Away. When your time is worth more than the few dollars you could pay to someone else to handle tasks, *pay them.* Okay, so it feels like a lot of out-of-pocket dollars. You're worth it!

In any urban or suburban area today, if you peruse the classified ads, shoppers' newsletters, and library and community bulletin boards, you can find nearly every service conceivable, such as:

❏ *Rent-a-Husband*—handyman services for around the house.
❏ *Errands Unlimited*—pickup and delivery by the hour.
❏ *Fine for Parking*—fights the city traffic bureau for you.
❏ *Tele-grocery*—all the food fit to bag, to your door.
❏ *Shall I Gift-Wrap It?*—expert, professional shopping services.
❏ *Garage on Wheels*—auto repair services that come to you.
❏ *The Maid Brigade*—cleans your house quickly and reliably.
❏ *Charge-a-Laser*—picks up and drops off printer and copier cartridges.
❏ *Clutter Bugs*—organizes your clutter so even you can find it.

❏ *Windows on the World*—have ladder, will wash windows on second floor.
❏ *Fast Mac*—home-based word-processing services.
❏ *Walking the Dog*—Rover's best friend while you're away.

Look for Ways to Make Your Work Count Twice. What activities do you undertake that can be made use of more than once?

Part of Marie's job involved giving speeches to community groups. One night, Marie taped her speech and had it transcribed. Later, she got back eighteen pages. Marie made her work count twice; she took three hours to fashion an article out of her speech. In a few months, she got it published.

Marie's husband, John wanted to upgrade his vocabulary skills but didn't have the urge to read a book or take a course. And he found the task painstakingly slow. John solved his problem by adding a dictionary software program to his hard disk.

Now, when he writes reports and wants to use a different word, with two keystrokes a variety of synonyms appear on his screen. John has made his work count twice—he writes better reports and increases his vocabulary each day.

Avoiding the IDITWE Syndrome. (IDITWE: I'll do it this weekend). Do you let errands pile up and then spend the weekend completing them? Instead of tying up a Saturday or Sunday, designate Monday evening from 7 to 10 P.M. or Thursday evening from 5 to 9 P.M. as errand night.

Most businesses are open for extended hours. While dressed and in your car, there is no better opportunity to make the rounds.

Handle Errands in Units. Take all your repairs to the tailor at once. Pay all your bills, if possible, at once. Consider paying two months in advance, forgoing the small amount of interest (had you placed the money in an interest-bearing account). Reduce the number of "pay the bills" evenings.

FRESH AIR: Preserve your weekends for recreational activities. You're worth it.

Beelines. To fully pursue an activity, make a beeline—the shortest path you can take. If you read about a new and helpful way to do something, use the technique immediately.

One executive says that when he encounters an idea for accomplishing a task that is superior to techniques he is currently using, he incorporates the new idea immediately. Rapid adoption avoids having the new idea linger and then die of neglect.

If something energizes you, provides peace of mind, or enables you to gain completions, incorporate it *now*.

Managing the Scraps to Gain Completion. What are "scraps"? Tidbits of information you wish to retain, coming to you from any source. The phone number of a good plumber, the name of the movie theater with the $2.50 matinees, and a poem you saw in a magazine qualify as scraps. In this era, we've all got dozens of scraps.

Holding scraps for too long or not allocating them appropriately clogs your intake capacity, and often results in losing them.

To quickly handle a scrap of information that enters your life, act on the scrap, whatever it is, right now or place it in a tickler file or a scraps notebook, to be acted upon when you pull those files. Don't let that scrap linger in your wallet or on your desk.

FRESH AIR: Deal with scraps quickly or risk not following through on the original reason you retained them. I find it convenient to convert scraps to on-location Post-it notes, which can be placed near the stove, near the medicine chest, on my car's dashboard, or at any of the other stations in my life.

Human Energy Zappers. Which individuals leave you exhausted and drained after a few minutes' conversation? Do you know coworkers, neighbors, or relatives who often complain when you speak to them? It will help to avoid them.

Edible Energy Zappers. Foods, as well as people and activities, can zap your energy and diminish your productivity. The rise of pizza delivery services directly contributes to sluggishness—eating heavy foods, and too much of them, for lunch causes a predictable slump as your body diverts its energy to breaking them down.

Coffee may be king of morning beverages and a "pick-me-up" throughout the day, but it cannot compete with a glass of sparkling, clear water to aid your performance. To be frank, coffee is a drug, as well as a harsh, acidic substance to be pouring down your throat.

Fast-food restaurants offer a false promise of speed, McDonald's in particular. You get in and out quickly, but the foods served, heavily laden with fats, sugars, and salts, rob you of vitality.

If you're serious about having more breathing space, give up chemically loaded burgers, greasy fries, and coconut-oil-based "shakes," *forever.*

Open-ended Period. Unless you have a deadline, and hence no choice, the hour of completion for new activities often cannot be accurately estimated. When possible, leave an open-ended period. Adopt the attitude "I am going to start at X o'clock and continue until finished."

By choosing this approach, your mission becomes successfully completing your task, not battling the clock. You will often finish sooner than expected and with energy to spare.

Hiding the clock supports an open-ended period. When something is important, hiding the clock enables you to harness your own internal rhythms and energy flow.

Liza dreaded the task of adding up her receipts, bills, and other items to complete her income taxes.

Early one March Saturday, she covered the clocks in her house, arranged all her receipts, and tackled the project head-on.

She knew when she started, but soon lost track of the hour. Later, she finished and put all of the receipts and paperwork into appropriate files. Then she looked at the clock. It was 11:39 A.M.

This monumental task that Liza had been dreading for weeks took less than three hours, including two bathroom breaks, one food break, several minutes gazing from her balcony, and several daydreams. By hiding the clock, she was able to fully engage in the task and gain mastery of her morning. Most people are far too concerned with what the clock says, rather than dealing with what is before them.

You can avoid looking at the clock more often during the work week than you think. If you've got an appointment, that's one thing, but when you're on a solo mission, that's another.

You can also "hide the clock" while relaxing. During a day's outing, leave your watch at home, don't bring the newspaper or other reading material, and refuse to talk shop with anyone.

Create Time Warps. This is my favorite suggestion in the whole book. It's related to hiding the clock. The more finely you schedule your tasks and activities, the more you use clocks to monitor your pace. This disrupts your own natural energy flow.

Have you ever experienced the feeling of being in a time warp? This occurs when you get so much accomplished, or your thoughts flow so freely, that seemingly many more hours have passed than actually have.

Time warps occur when you are not conscious of your output or responsiveness in relationship to fixed intervals, such as an hour. You are proceeding at your internal pace, WHICH CANNOT BE EQUATED WITH MAN-MADE INTERVALS.

You can increase the likelihood of experiencing a favorable time warp effect by removing yourself from the time-measured environment—by hiding the clock. This is why working on a park bench, in an airplane seat, or on your back porch often yields far greater output than anticipated or accomplished during the same interval while at a desk in a traditional office.

One hour of uncluttered thought can yield more benefits than days of common desk work.

FRESH AIR: Throughout the day, there may be stretches to do your best work free from the confines of the clock. As you become more comfortable *not* watching a clock, you'll notice that your orientation to time begins to shift. You'll complete tasks with far greater ease.

As you become more focused on the activities you undertake, you will be less inclined to want to have a clock in sight.

Isolation by Choice

Often, you create situations in which you are facing a crunch. Regardless, when you have resolved that no disturbances in completing your task will be tolerated, condition your environment for *no* distractions.

You could barricade yourself in a room and post warning signs; take the far cubbyhole on the third floor of the library; or find any remote location where you avoid distracting influences. Again, you can accomplish in hours what otherwise might require a week.

Q: It sounds like a luxury to be able to allocate six or eight hours just like that. How many people can actually do this?

A: Nearly everyone has some discretion over how she will complete a task. If you have to leave your office to complete something, most bosses understand.

In advance, identify those places where you will be able to work steadily, when you choose to:

The conference room	A coworker's office
The library	The attic or basement
The back porch	A hotel room
The car, while parked	A picnic table

You'll know when you've found the right spot. You feel good, productive, and unhurried.

Creative Procrastination

——

Those who make the worst use of their time are the first to complain of its brevity.
—JEAN DE LA BRUYÈRE,
17TH-CENTURY FRENCH WRITER

——

It would be a wonderful world if you could always tackle the most important projects first thing in the morning. Unfortunately, you don't, and sometimes cannot, work that way. Some days you can't *make* yourself get started on the task at hand. We all procrastinate much more than we care to admit. Let's take a quick look at how to *harness* procrastination.

My approach to procrastination is that if I am handling other priority and goal-related tasks or activities, nothing is lost. Afterward, the task or activity that I have put off still has to be done. The difference is that when I am ready to begin the task I had put off, I have gotten other things out of the way.

160

In a sense, creative procrastination is a form of activity shifting, like using a VCR to tape a show and watch it later.

Hold on, pard'ner! I am not recommending that you procrastinate. When you can't get started on the task at hand, however, take care of something else important.

Techniques for Breaking Through Procrastination

Face Procrastination Head-on. Ask yourself what is blocking you, what is the real reason you don't want to get started. Write it down or record it on cassette. This exercise may dislodge something and help you to begin.

Choose to Easily Begin. Make a positive affirmation to yourself: "I choose to easily begin on this task." Making this formal choice has power and often is enough to get you started.

Employ the Three-to-five Method. Ask yourself, "What are three to five things I could do, not to tackle the project headlong, but just to dabble a bit?" Then initiate these "easy entry" activities. Often they are enough to get you started headlong on the project.

Ready or Not. I've found that sometimes the best way to get started is simply to turn the PC on (or whatever else I'm working with). When the darn thing is ready, saints and begorra, I'm ready.

Jump Starting. Jump starting often enables you to capture your first and sometimes best thoughts. Suppose it's Friday afternoon. You have a project to start on Monday. You don't want to initiate the project now, but you would like to be ready on Monday.

Using jump starting, you might preview any supporting items, jot down some notes, begin a rough outline, or undertake other supporting activities now, "while it doesn't count."

In the pre-initiation stage—Friday afternoon, before the project "starts"—your ideas and thoughts can flow freely. This ten-minute period can be valuable in facilitating how Monday goes, when it does count. Your subconscious starts working on the project. By Monday, you are "raring to go."

Overcoming Procrastination on Big Projects

When working on a long-term goal, it's easy to lose momentum, or feel as if you will never achieve it, especially for goals stretching over several years or more. Use the *day unit* as a convenient measure for charting progress in pursuit of your goals.

How does the day unit work? First, consider that:

❑ John F. Kennedy was president for 1,037 days;

❑ Columbus crossed the Atlantic in seventy-one days.

For large goals, begin thinking in day units. A day unit equals six hours of concentrated, focused work in a calendar day. Why six hours? With concentrated, focused work, six hours is plenty. Leave yourself two hours for conditioning your environment, managing the beforehand, and filing.

Calculate how many day units you'll need to reach a long-term goal. Factor in the weekends, holidays, and other downtime. The figure you derive will be a manageable, meaningful unit by which your long-term goals can be approached. Knowing you have a 275-day task ahead of you can help reduce anxiety today.

Approached with perspective, procrastination can lead to creativity and new approaches to big tasks.

Now, let's turn the corner to metaphysical tools for living and working at a comfortable pace in a sped-up society.

PART
V

METAPHYSICAL
TOOLS

Living in the Moment

Right now is the most important moment in your life.
—ROBERT FRITZ, FOUNDER,
TECHNOLOGIES FOR CREATING

What are you waiting for before you're willing to fully engage in life, in this day?

- ❏ The winning lotto ticket?
- ❏ Your name in lights?
- ❏ A big raise or promotion?
- ❏ A female president?
- ❏ Your children to grow up?
- ❏ The big quake?
- ❏ Recognition? Respect?
- ❏ Christmas? An apology?
- ❏ Spring? Earth Day?
- ❏ A rainy day? A sunny day?
- ❏ Someday?

Years ago, following one of his lectures in class, a young lady left a piece of paper on Professor Leo Buscaglia's desk. On the page was a poem entitled, "Things You Didn't Do."

Remember the day I borrowed your brand new car and I dented it? I thought you'd kill me. But you didn't.

And remember the time I dragged you to the beach and you said it would rain, and it did? I thought you'd say, "I told you so." But you didn't.

Do you remember the time I flirted with all the guys to make you jealous, and you were? I thought you'd leave me. But you didn't.

Do you remember the time I spilled blueberry pie all over your car rug? I thought you'd hit me, but you didn't.

And remember the time I forgot to tell you that the dance was formal and you showed up in jeans? I thought you'd smack me. But you didn't.

Yes, there were lots of things you didn't do, but you put up with me, and you loved me, and you protected me.

There were lots of things I wanted to make up to you when you returned from Vietnam. But you didn't.

Living, Loving & Learning by Leo F. Buscaglia © 1982, SLACK, Inc. Reprinted with permission.

What does "living in the moment" mean? It means living with vibrant expression and keen perception, with an intense awareness of what exists in your life. It's waking up each morning with the thought "I'm alive, and this day is only starting."

Living in the moment means being aware of your power in the present; it is not a recipe for accomplishment. It is observing the finely woven canvas of your life while you are also living it.

It is giving yourself permission to be who you are. It is resting when you are tired. It is not having to strive. It is allowing yourself breathing space.

No False Approaches. Living in the moment does not mean taking a Pollyanna approach to life, pretending that all is well. *All* is never well, with anyone, at least for long. Living in the moment doesn't mean acquiring a façade. You don't have to cheerfully greet everyone you pass.

Freed from the preoccupation that limits your experience of the present, however, you may feel like greeting everyone.

Living in the moment does not mean living for the moment or living to get to the next moment. It means total, unconditional acknowledgment that what is *now*, *is* your life; that *now* is the only moment there is.

Not that you can't work to change things, but that right now, this is how things are. For most people, often, how things are is not so bad, and how things can be *is* in reach.

Living for the moment does not mean "Live for

today"—a well-intentioned but shortsighted philosophy. Some time management experts suggest pretending you only have six months to live. The exercise misses the mark, however. It would be silly to sell off your property and spend down your savings if you have years left to live. Living in the moment encompasses the truth about your life.

It does not mean "Get the most out of life"; there is no "most" to get. It does not mean "Make every minute count"—an attitude that borders on obsessiveness.

Lost in the Overglut

Although the concept of living in the moment is primal, it is needed now more than ever. Too few individuals have any experience or knowledge of living in the moment. It is lost in a flurry of activity, "busy-ness." The overglut strangles it. Living in the moment remains one of the least understood, least addressed, least used human capabilities.

Several decades ago, Alan Watts explored living in the moment in his book *The Wisdom of Insecurity*. He observed, "Human beings appear to be happy" when they have something to look forward to. Yet, when that something arrives, "it is difficult to enjoy it to the full without some promise of more to come." The relentless quest to move on to what's next keeps you and me from fully enjoying what's here.

Certainly, one can look forward with anticipation to future events, and can hold fond memories or learn valuable lessons from the past. Preoccupation, however, is elongated deliberation of what came before or what may be. Preoccupation with the past, or future, blocks experience of the present.

Barbara, driving down the main road of a nearby city, barely perceives being with her new boyfriend while she recounts what went wrong when she was here last year with her ex-boyfriend.

Roger's lingering anticipation of a better future diminishes his ability to address his less-than-acceptable present.

Do you reminisce about something or someone in your past, perhaps with nostalgia, even though, back then, the experience was not nearly as pleasant? For reasons of adaptation, our memories selectively retain positive elements of certain experiences.

You fantasize about that boyfriend, or girlfriend, of several years ago with whom you *knew* there was no chance of having a successful relationship. Yet, you only partially experience the present with your spouse, who is among the most wonderful human beings you know.

A writer once remarked that after his father's death, his father's absence became much greater than his presence. "When he was alive," the writer said, "he wasn't especially present in my life. When I went about my business, I felt neither his presence nor his absence."

FRESH AIR: Longing more strongly for what you no longer have, rather than reveling in what you do have, is a guarantee that you will miss the present and all the magic *it* holds. Revel in what you have.

Often, when a parent dies, the surviving adult children are finally able to see the beauty and perfection of the parent's life. Yet, these aspects were there to see all along. So, too, the beauty and perfection of your own life are available for you to see, right now.

FRESH AIR: Do five years have to pass before you can regard today with fondness? Can you accept that *right now* your life is taking place? Can you shout for joy for no reason? Can you give your love unconditionally?

IF YOU'RE EVER GOING TO LOVE ME

If you're ever going to love me,
   love me now, while I can know
   all the sweet and tender feelings
   from which real affection flow.

Love me now, while I am living,
   don't wait until I'm gone,
   and then chisel it in marble—
   warm words of love on ice cold stone.

If you have sweet thoughts about me,
   why not whisper them to me?
   Don't you know they would make me
     happy,
   and as glad as glad could be?

If you wait 'til I am sleeping,
   never to wake here again,
   there'll be walls of earth between us
   and I couldn't hear you then . . .

I won't need your kind caresses
   when the grass grows o'er my face;
   I won't crave your love or kisses
   in my last low resting place.

So, then, if you love me any,
   if it's but a little bit,
   let me know it now while living;
   I can own and treasure it

                    (Unknown)

Back to the Present

For a toddler, no other moment exists but the present. You cannot trade her world for yours, but you can embark now on the quest to live in the moment. Marshall McLuhan says, "There is absolutely no inevitably as long as there is a willingness to contemplate what is happening."

Adam sat at his desk for yet another evening, inspecting what he had to finish before retiring.

Out of nowhere, a great notion came to him: If he was ever to experience a complete, fulfilled, stress-free life, it would have to be moment to moment, and it would have to start right now.

He could no longer pretend that his life would change when his desired future finally arrived. And, he realized he could not store up relaxation or rest, like squirrels storing acorns for the winter.

Right now was everything; if right now was not fine, he would deal with it now.

Good or bad, the present moment is, in reality, all you have. It is the only point of power, the only moment in which action can be taken. Your ability to acknowledge and to live within it is a basic, satisfying human capability.

Living in the moment is the hallmark of people with breathing space.

Blocked Experiences

Living in the moment is freedom to experience
the essence and perfection of your life and what is
now, even aspects you may not like about *now*.

Today, as the mass media flood us with images of
perfection, increasingly we find that we are discon-
tent with ourselves at a fundamental level—our bod-
ies. Among men, more than half would like to
change their weight. Nearly one in three desires one
or more of the following: to have more muscles,
better teeth, more hair, more height, or no signs of
aging.

Among women, more than three out of four are
nearly obsessed with weight. One-third want to lose
more than twenty-five pounds. Varying percentages
would like to change their thighs, buttocks, teeth,
hair, bust, or entire physique, and so on.

Each of us faces many obstacles to living in the
moment and having a full experience of the present.
Beyond battling the overglut, striving—characterized by overachieving and constantly exerting extra
effort, encouraged in our society—will keep you
from this moment.

FRESH AIR: There is no evidence that strivers
rise faster in their careers than those who maintain
a healthy, steady pace. You don't have to rush to

catch up or get ahead, because you're not behind. You simply are where you are, and you can make choices about where you want to be.

Clinging to victim status helps one avoid personal responsibility for existing in the present. Not making completions or having poor transitions between activities yields the perception of not having enough time.

Too much noise can block your experience; you need some quiet. Drugs and alcohol block the present and offer distortions. I suspect that perceived time-pressure is the reason that legions of our society have turned to drugs and alcohol.

Failure to live in the moment condemns you to never feeling in control of your life.

FRESH AIR: The breakthrough of a lifetime: accepting the present moment as it is, and for what it is—the most important moment in your life. How fortunate if you're happy or content *right now*, because *now* has the greatest importance. Nothing else exists.

Getting to the Now

Some experiences, such as finding love, suffering the death of someone close, graduating, relocating, celebrating a birthday or anniversary, or a particularly moving event, throw us into the present, ready or not. They tend to make us appreciate what we have.

The same holds true when looking down from a mountain or a window seat on a plane several miles up. (Then, too often, we jump in a taxi at the airport and lose the power of the moment.)

We've all experienced the strange mixture of heightened sensation and temporary alteration or cessation of time. Why? Who knows, but probably because we have an expanded view of the occasion, as we rarely do during the daily humdrum.

You don't have to wait for these kinds of experiences. To live in the moment, to get to now, start with the truth, be authentic. Without lingering, candidly describe your life to yourself. Include: career, finances, peace of mind, social status, aspirations, disappointments, shortcomings, triumphs, opportunities, and challenges.

If you have a camcorder and VCR, film yourself. The experience is likely to be moving. It also can serve as an historical benchmark of the way you were.

Concentrate on your breathing. This allows you to stop and contemplate who you are and where you are. I find it helpful to say my name, today's date, and how I feel: "I'm Jeff Davidson, it's October 12, and I feel very fit." It helps to find a quiet space and allow everything to slow down.

Some fine morning this week, arise at 5:30 A.M. and take a walk. Rise and shine and claim this morning. Witness the sunrise. Embrace a new day on earth and in your life.

As often as you can, have close encounters with nature—waterfalls, the crispness of freshly fallen leaves, thunderstorms, and ocean waves all spark our sense of aliveness and stimulate our creative capacities.

Actively seek experiences for renewal in your life. Take a different path. Call that long-lost friend. Extend yourself in ways that surprise you.

Staying Present. To stay present, continually acknowledge others for their input into your life. Gain more space to *be* by giving others space to be; for one week acknowledge anything that anyone does for you. Your words can offer the most heartfelt expression of human emotion, or simple recognition: "Terry, I want to acknowledge you for your efforts on the project this week."

Last, but not least, simply sit quietly in your home or office, perhaps in a chair you don't often use. You may find it hard to relax at first, and understandably so. The message we get from the mega-realities is to go faster and faster. Simply notice what you've collected and how you've arranged things. Notice your life.

Stillness, the antithesis of a fast-forward existence, is underrated. A few moments of stillness each day help you to fully experience now. Stillness fosters breathing space.

IF I HAD MY LIFE TO LIVE OVER
by Nadine Starr, age 85—October 1975

I'd dare to make more mistakes next time.
I'd relax. I would limber up.
I would be sillier than I have been this trip.
I would take fewer things seriously.
I would take more chances. I would take more
    trips.
I would climb more mountains and swim more
    rivers.
I would eat more ice-cream and less beans.
I would perhaps have more actual troubles, but
    I'd have fewer imaginary ones.

You see, I'm one of those people who live sensi-
    bly and sanely
Hour after hour, day after day.
Oh, I've had my moments and if I had it to do
    over again I'd have more of them. In fact, I'd
    try to have nothing else.
Just moments.
One after another, instead of living so many
    years ahead of each day.
I've been one of those persons who never goes
    anywhere without a
Thermometer, a hot water bottle, a raincoat,
    and a parachute.
If I had to do it again, I would travel lighter
    than I have.

If I had my life to live over, I would start bare-

foot earlier in the Spring
And stay that way later in the Fall.

I would go to more dances.
I would ride more merry-go-rounds.
I would pick more daisies.

Nadine

Choosing Breathing Space

Man must not allow the clock and the calendar to blind him to the fact that each moment of his life is a miracle and a mystery.
—H. G. WELLS, SCIENCE FICTION AUTHOR

You're stalled in traffic on the interstate highway, on a sweltering day in August, when your car air conditioner conks out. On top of that, today you happen to be wearing a wool tweed suit with no underwear. Do you feel justified in being irritated? Other choices are available.

You could choose to acknowledge the good life you're leading; hum your favorite song; or remember when you've been stuck before and how the ordeal was of no consequence the next day.

You could be glad that you live in this country; about what's planned for dinner this evening; or that your kids are healthy. How you elect to feel is always your choice. The act of choosing is a simple but powerful technique that will further aid you in attaining breathing space.

Robert Fritz teaches that by making choices, positive affirmations to yourself regarding what you want, you move closer each day to attaining them. This is not synonymous with "positive thinking." The choices Fritz suggests are made regularly, regardless of how you feel at the moment you're making them. Your goal is to keep making them.

> Making deeply pronounced choices is an efficient way to get in control of life and experience an abundance of breathing space.

An essential choice for maintaining breathing space is choosing to feel worthy and complete, simply spoken to yourself: "I choose to feel worthy and complete." This helps you to reduce anxiety, stay calm, and feel more relaxed.

Depending on how long it's been since you've felt worthy and complete, you may have to make this choice for many days or weeks running. But keep at it.

By choosing to feel worthy and complete, you automatically redirect the inner and outer you to accept that there is nothing you must do or must finish. Everything is based on your choice.

If you choose to continue working on some task, even one assigned to you, the choice is made in the present moment, not based on a prior agenda. A worthy and complete feeling yields a tremendous sense of inner harmony.

Choosing to Trust Yourself. A study in the 1940s of highly successful people found, uniformly, that they reached decisions quickly and retreated from them slowly, if ever. A more recent study reveals that when people make decisions based on instinct, they end up happier than those who make decisions based on careful analysis.

Hmm. Too much thinking could be hazardous to your choices, and to your happiness.

Choosing to trust yourself, and to trust your ability to choose, is the antidote to relying on time-consuming information crutches. Trusting yourself enhances your ability to choose based on limited information. "I choose to trust my ability to make the right choice," even with limited information.

Recall when your past hunches proved correct. It probably happened frequently. Hereafter, why not recognize and accept your built-in mechanism for self-direction?

FRESH AIR: In the larger sense, accept that you don't need to expose yourself to the daily deluge of the over-information era to make appropriate choices. More often than you may realize, you already have the tools you need.

When determining what activities to retain and what to drop, don't be afraid to trust your feelings. They exist for a purpose and often guide you well.

Choosing to Feel at Home. Years ago when Maria Shriver was co-hosting one of the morning TV shows in New York, she would fly in each week from her home in California, and return at the end of the week. Crisscrossing the United States on nearly 100 trips per year is a considerable amount of travel, not to mention disruption.

Shriver minimized the effects of thousands of miles in the air, and still maintained balance. Each Friday evening, when heading back to California, she took the same flight, at the same airport, on the same airline, leaving the same gate, at the same hour. She even reserved the same seat.

She often flew with the same pilots and same flight crew, and, occasionally, the same passengers. Rather than having to be physically back at her house or touching down at the Los Angeles airport, she felt at home when she boarded the plane. In essence, she minimized the effects of a rigorous schedule by transforming her seat in the sky into a welcomed sanctuary. She was home in that seat.

Likewise, you can feel at home without having to be at home. Choosing to feel at home (when you are not) enhances your sense of breathing space. Think of it, the opportunity to be fully present in places where you might otherwise have been thinking more about being elsewhere.

FRESH AIR: Choosing to feel at home frees you to experience the present moment, with its surrounding scenery, to the fullest. Given no fear for safety, some human beings can feel at home anywhere on earth.

Choosing, Rather Than Reacting

Reacting and responding are weak tools with which to gain control of your life. Worse, they disarm your power to choose.

FRESH AIR: Determine how you feel right now or at any given moment. If you are angry, notice that you are angry; if you are embarrassed, notice that. By giving vent to your present emotions, you help release blocked energy and gain a fuller sense of the present. You have more control over how you choose to feel.

By continuing to make positive choices, you can preserve and broaden your sense of breathing space. Below are but a few examples of the choices you can make in the various aspects of your life.

Note that all the choices are worded to indicate what you want to have, not what you wish to avoid. Maintain this distinction clearly when formulating your own choices. Choosing by avoidance yields little power. Directly addressing what you want or how you want to feel yields great power:

Quality of Life

I choose to live in the moment.
I choose to easily have breathing space.
I choose to enjoy my life.
I choose to easily acknowledge my completions
   each day.

I choose to feel comfortable wherever I am.

I choose to maintain balance and harmony.
I choose to live a clutter-free existence.
I choose to acknowledge that time is my ally.
I choose to get a good night's sleep, every night.
I choose to easily remain organized.

I choose to feel comfortable in the face of
uncertainty.
I choose to remain true to myself.
I choose to be a vibrant and radiant being.
I choose to approach each day with enthusiasm.
I choose to revel in what I have.

Social Life and Leisure

I choose to feel good about how I spend
my days.
I choose to be with my friends often.
I choose to enjoy my vacations.
I choose to make new friends easily.
I choose to engage in rewarding new
experiences.

I choose to be a good companion and a good
listener.
I choose to relax easily.
I choose to enjoy new experiences.
I choose to sometimes do nothing.
I choose to take time off freely for myself.

I choose to return to work feeling energized.
I choose to acknowledge my sexiness.

I choose to be playful.
I choose to feel totally comfortable with myself.
I choose to get newer each day.

Health

I choose to maintain a balanced diet.
I choose to maintain a trim, fit body.
I choose to have a strong, healthy heart.
I choose to thrive on challenging situations.
I choose to always maintain a healthy outlook.

I choose to get annual checkups.
I choose to feel better each day.
I choose to have strong, healthy lungs.
I choose to get a good night's sleep every night.
I choose to awake each morning refreshed
    and alert.

I choose to maintain a harmonious balance in
    my life.
I choose to continuously draw strong, deep
    breaths.
I choose to live a long, happy life.
I choose to maintain a cheerful outlook.
I choose to simply feel good.

Work Life

I choose to educate myself continually.
I choose to easily and continually stay informed
    of the key issues in my field.
I choose to handle easily the challenges I face.

I choose to remain awake and alert at work.
I choose to have fun at work and at play.

I choose to easily work well with others.
I choose to maintain high productivity all day.
I choose to build momentum toward goals.
I choose to easily have endurance.
I choose to form powerful unions with
    coworkers.

I choose to make new choices as needed.
I choose to easily accept the input of others.
I choose to accept my role as a leader.
I choose to serve my boss/clients/constituents
    well.
I choose to leave work feeling energized.

Handling Success

I choose to acknowledge my completions
    frequently.
I choose to acknowledge my accomplishments,
    big and small.
I choose to easily gain the recognition and re-
    wards I deserve.
I choose to easily manage the abundance that is
    forthcoming to me.
I choose to become even more skilled at what
    I do.

I choose to become a mentor to others.
I choose to remain humble.
I choose to be open to new ways of doing things.

I choose to share my success with others.

I choose to acknowledge the accomplishments of others.

I choose to stay connected to the creative process.

I choose to experience unlimited happiness.

I choose to easily retain that which supports me.

I choose to reach for the highest that is within me.

I choose to maintain clarity in my work and my life.

Family

I choose to freely be with my family.

I choose to easily meet my financial obligations and support my family.

I choose to further the education of my children.

I choose to acknowledge members of my family every day.

I choose to actively support my family's interests.

I choose to easily give and receive love.

I choose to give others the space to be.

I choose to have high energy for my family.

I choose to be responsive to my family's needs.

I choose to listen passionately to my family.

Personal Development

I choose to embody calmness and serenity.

I choose to be an active listener to others.
I choose to embody grace and ease.
I choose to embody patience and understanding.
I choose to feel at ease.

I choose to embody tolerance, kindness, and
warmth.
I choose to easily acknowledge others.
I choose to smile often.
I choose to look for the humor in my life.
I choose to accept others as they are.

I choose to easily speak for myself.
I choose to be empowered by others.
I choose to hold positive thoughts exclusively.
I choose to embrace the present moment.
I choose to accept myself as I am.

Ability to Handle Change

I choose to follow my own inner wisdom.
I choose to easily make decisions.
I choose to have clarity.
I choose to easily build change into my long-
term plans.
I choose to readily respond to appropriate
change.

I choose to accept change with high energy and
enthusiasm.
I choose to take action readily on new ideas.
I choose to identify problems and resolve them.
I choose to discover the opportunity in
adversity.

I choose to be open to new points of view.

Planetary

I choose to support a clean environment.
I choose to celebrate the diversity of life on the
    planet.
I choose to respect plant and animal life.
I choose to lend my interest and support to XYZ
    cause.
I choose to make a worthwhile contribution to
    the planet.

I choose to support integrity among nations.
I choose to support world peace.

Choices and priorities can go hand in hand; a priority is a choice that is prevalent in your life.

Maintaining Your Choices

As with any quest to reinforce choices you make, write or type your choices and post them, or record them on cassette and play them back. Choose what feels right for you, and keep choosing. While you're waiting in a bank line, run through your choices. If you notice yourself wavering, recall the new behavior or feeling that you've chosen.

You can choose to overcome rituals that no longer support you, or you can make choices beyond anything others would have guessed you'd ever choose.

A new idea is such a rare thing. Often we simply parrot what we hear or read. *You can make choices that are not congruent with your history.* You can make choices that no one has ever made before.

Go beyond the choices suggested above and devise those that uniquely serve your purposes, that will give the best and most lasting chance for breathing space.

Handling Breakdowns. Breakdowns, when nothing seems to be going right, are a recurring fact of life. They represent lost power in the present. They are, however, disguised opportunities to reinforce your choices.

Examine your day. Where are the familiar bottlenecks or slow periods? Where do you feel cramped for breathing space? What new choices can you make?

When you get off course, redirect your energies. Pat McCallum, a human development trainer in Chevy Chase, Maryland, suggests asking the question "What do I want right now?" If you ask that question and listen closely to yourself, the answer that is right for you can emerge.

Go for a walk if you're stymied. Remove yourself from your present environment and walk around the block, or to the nearest park. Often you come back with a new perspective and a readiness to get started again.

Occasionally, the only way to handle a breakdown is to exit from a quiet space and jump into the fray: get involved, volunteer, help out on a deadline.

You will be amazed at how jumping into an activity can get you past a breakdown.

If you're really stuck, talk to people who can help—a mentor, a friend, a spouse, anyone who knows you well enough or knows how to get you back in the saddle.

When Not to Choose. Choosing works best for issues important to you, for how you want to feel or for what you want to accomplish. Recognizing the overabundance of choices in our society, it's best not to get caught up investing energy in making low-level choices.

FRESH AIR: Most decisions you could make are of little consequence. *Not choosing* can be restful, comforting, even refreshing. It can also open up new possibilities. "Honey, you decide where we'll go this evening."

Choose when it matters; let go when it doesn't.

22

Breathing Space for All

Teach that which you wish to master.

Long after the zenith of Greek society, the world continued to admire Greek contributions to literature, the arts, philosophy, and science. To emulate the Greeks was considered to be in good taste. To this day, the Golden Age of Greece is revered as one of the most splendid eras in human history.

As with much of history, a great deal is lost or altered over the ages. In the Greek city-state of Sparta, for example, during its heyday in the fifth century B.C., the typical Greek citizen was served by *twenty* slaves. They rendered their masters all kinds of breathing space to devote to whatever they wanted.

Thankfully, no one today has dominion over others. If you are a head of state, an executive, or the parent of three cooperative teenagers, you can dele-

194

gate much of what you face to gain more breathing space for yourself.

If you're like most people, more often than not, you have to rely on number one to get things done . . . and that's fine, because you can handle it.

As we've seen throughout this book, you don't have to allow the overglut, the lack of clear priorities and goals, or negative choices to impede you. *There are* people who more often than not have the breathing space they need to live and work at a comfortable pace. I'm lucky enough to be among them.

I didn't start out that way, but by trial and tribulation, and inquiry and examination, all of which led to **Breathing Space**, I found it is possible to live and work at a comfortable pace most of the time. Yes, I do feel pressured and overwhelmed occasionally, but those feelings rarely last beyond the immediate present. Now you know, they no longer need to last with you either.

A Wider View

Let's focus on enhancing breathing space from a broader perspective. We have explored the ways in which we get caught up in the overglut and choices in our society. We have replaced them with ways in which to maintain control, including:

Establishing priorities and setting goals;
  Aligning daily activities;
    Conditioning your environments;

Managing the beforehand;
Controlling the intake overglut;
Giving yourself completions;
Acknowledging yourself and others;
Living in the present moment;
Choosing what you want and how to feel.

Already you feel a growing sense of confidence in your ability to attain breathing space, and to make time your ally. Yet, there is a larger challenge awaiting you.

In the world to come, it's conceivable that all nations will become open and democratic societies. Thereafter, a valid measure of freedom will be the freedom to address the problems confronting our planet and development as a species. We can't get to this higher agenda if great masses of our population continue daily to rake through the morass of the over-information era.

The Danger of Accommodation. Professor John Kenneth Galbraith studied poverty-stricken societies on four different continents over several years. In his book *The Nature of Mass Poverty*, he concluded that the reason some societies remain poor, century after century, is that they *accommodate* poverty.

Galbraith found that as difficult as it is for people to live in abject poverty, they are not willing to accept the difficulty of making a better life for themselves.

Our society appears poised to *accommodate* the overglut, as if this is the way it's always been and the way it must be. Singularly, and in unison, our ticket to more breathing space is to refuse to accommodate the overglut.

Individually and collectively, the primary issue before us is attaining a clutter-free society. The larger issues of environmental clutter and the long-term vitality of the earth are directly related.

I don't want to be part of a decaying society of individuals who can't manage their own spaces or the spaces common to everyone. I don't want to live in a society or a world of time-pressed people who have nothing left to give future generations. My guess is that you don't either.

I choose to live in a society composed of people leading balanced lives with rewarding careers, happy home lives, and enough space to enjoy themselves, and I choose to live in *this* society.

The pace of life for much of the world will speed up even more. The future will belong to those nations populated by individuals who steadfastly choose to maintain control of their lives, effectively draw upon their resourcefulness and imagination, and teach others around them to do the same.

Individually and collectively, we need to preserve and expand upon our sense of breathing space, so that we have the energy, creativity, and resolve to meet the challenges that we face, and greater challenges forthcoming.

We need to attain breathing space for ourselves and then to teach others. For the good of all, we need to freely share new perspectives. We owe it to ourselves and to those who come after us.

AFTERWORD

It's easy to feel lost in the swamp and underbrush of our daily existence. **Breathing Space** has offered an assortment of exciting ideas and a practical action plan to new order, energy, and meaning in one's life. By following the principles in this book, you have a legitimate route up to the mountain peak of achievement and fulfillment.

The practical "Fresh Air" tips will enable you to maintain that vantage point and enjoy your life. Whether you are besieged with paper or attempting to cut a swath through too much on your plate, the guidance you need is offered here.

As Jeff Davidson appropriately described, the overglut is relentless; each day we must recognize how we let it creep into our lives and dominate us. Keeping the spaces in your life clear leads to mastery and enjoyment of life.

As with all learning, one reading or one exposure to new ideas is usually not enough to embrace and then embody the principles offered. As such, I recommend that you skim through **Breathing Space** again and again after your initial reading, so that you increase the quality and duration of the breathing you attain each day.

Alan N. Schaifer,
Harvard Law School Association

APPENDIX

Slowing Down the Pace

Watch the clock for three minutes and then cover
it all day.
Close your eyes for sixty seconds and visualize
an enjoyable scene.
Eliminate three items from your "to do" list
without doing them.
With your eyes closed, listen to music with head-
phones.

Sit quietly and visualize or meditate.
Look at the ground intently from your airplane
seat.
Acknowledge your completions.
Choose to master your use of time.

Six Ways to Shake Up Your Routine

Get up without using an alarm clock.
Work on the porch, under a tree, or at the pool.
Work in your parked car when appropriate.

Review your mail on alternate days.
Hold all calls for two days.
Get ruthless, drop what doesn't support you.

Ten "C's" for Living at a Comfortable Pace

Constantly read your priorities and goals list.

Challenge and avoid your own ritual behavior.

Consider what would happen if you did not handle something.

Convincingly, but politely, say no.

Clear your desk of everything except the one task at hand.

Clear your files of deadwood.

Count twice—look for all the ways to reapply the work you have already done.

Create space by canceling the unnecessary.

Choose to feel at home when not.

Choose to get a good night's sleep every night.

NEW TERMS FOR A
MISUNDERSTOOD ERA

Acknowledging. Recognizing or giving credit to another who has been helpful or productive in some way. Tends to aid both the giver and receiver to live in the moment. Can also be used for the self. (See *Self-acknowledgment.*)

Active reading. Seeking material on a specific topic to enhance one's understanding and knowledge.

Backup system. Any system that, in the face of a breakdown, allows one to continue without delay. For example, if you keep a spare car key in your wallet, and if you accidentally lock yourself out, your backup system, in this case the key, enables you to proceed.

Band-Aid fix. A short-term approach to handling a problem. Usually is insufficient in the long run and may contribute to an even greater problem.

Beeline. The shortest route to integrating new data or new ways to proceed.

Breathing space. You know it when you have it. It is the feeling of having time and space, of being in control, or content, or relaxed. It is the room to be, to explore, or to do nothing.

Calendar block-back. A method for enhancing progress toward goals by starting from the ending date and plotting milestones up to the present.

Choosing. The most important concept for human effectiveness; offers new approaches to what competes for your attention and to gain breathing space.

Clock-chasing. A situation characterized by individuals or populations who find themselves in perpetual motion.

Complete. A state of being, separation from what came before.

Completions. An orientation to activities and life whereby accomplishments are experienced in divisible units. Greatly enhances the experience of breathing space.

Conditioning. Preparation and activities for responding to responsibilities and experiences.

Creating space. A perception that occurs when a scheduled event becomes unscheduled, or when a time warp occurs (see below).

Creative procrastination. Taking care of all other useful tasks while putting off an important or urgent task.

Creative trashing. Determining how much you can toss, and then doing it!

Davidson's Law. "Items competing for one's attention expand so as to fill the time and hinder work allocated for completion."

Deskmanship. The art of managing what is placed on and crosses one's desk.

Distractions. Anything that blocks effectiveness or the experience of the present moment.

Eyewitness report. A term used by local television news

to convince you to pay attention to the details of the latest fire or train derailment, etc.

Feeling at home. The ability to feel at home while commuting, at work, traveling, etc., brings a feeling of calmness and serenity normally experienced only when actually returning home.

Filing. The price we pay to remain organized in an information-overload society. Effective filing yields peace of mind.

Future file. A file for information whose value or use in the present is not readily seen.

Horizontal piles. An archaic, inefficient psuedo-system for storing information. No human being can effectively deal with horizontal piles.

Household loading dock. A shelf or table near or on the way to the front door that temporarily holds those items to be carried to a new post outside the home.

Information crutch. Any form of knowledge used by individuals to support present or future goals or activities. Highly plentiful in the information-overload age, and usually unnecessary.

Intake overglut, or **overglut.** The deluge of information and items that surround us.

Isolation by choice. A technique whereby one cuts off all communication with the outside world to devote full attention to a task or activity.

Jump start. Initiating a small portion of a project or activity in advance, so as to gain familiarity for when the project or activity actually begins.

Leisure. Traditionally, when one is free of tasks and activities directly related to employment. Its emerging definition is rest and relaxation, replenishment, revitalization.

Living in the moment. Continual realization that *now* is the only moment that exists.

Managing the beforehand. Living with the acknowledgment that change is continually forthcoming and preparing for it.

Now this . . . A verbal technique used by broadcasters to instantaneously shift the attention of viewers or listeners.

Open-ended. A concept in which a project is initiated at a specific time and proceeds with no specific ending time, with the understanding that as soon as it can be accomplished, it will be.

Organization. A tool for personal control.

Packratism. The tendency to overcollect.

Parkinson's Law. Stated as "Work expands to fill the time allotted for its completion," is *repealed* as of now.

Preoccupation. Consumed with thought. A block to living in the present moment.

Quality time. A lie, an erroneous notion propagated by those who are thwarted by the five mega-realities.

Self-acknowledgment. Giving yourself praise or recognition for a good job completion or other accomplishment.

Slowing down the clock. Any technique in which time

seems to be passing slowly. Staring at the clock or achieving sensory underload each slows down one's perception of passing time.

Standing in line. A near daily activity directly related to the density of the surrounding population and the availability of services.

Time. No one is sure; however, for too many people it has become a negative four-letter word.

Time-pressed, or **time pressure.** An abundance of goals, tasks, and activities and a dearth of resources for undertaking them.

Symbolic success. The outer trappings of success without the peace of mind to enjoy yourself.

Time Warp. The experience of accomplishment when proceeding at one's own internal pace; occurs more frequently by removing oneself from time-measured environments.

Wasted time. The perception that progress is being thwarted.

RECOMMENDED READING

Ball, Rick. *Making Space: Design for Compact Living.* New York: Overlook Press, 1990.

Bradbury, Ray. "Night Meeting," *The Martian Chronicles.* New York: Doubleday, 1946.

Buscaglia, Leo, Ph.D. *Living, Loving, Learning.* Thoroughfare, New Jersey, 1982.

Conner, Daryl. *Travelling with the Speed of Change.* New York: Villard, 1992.

Davidson, Jeff. *Power and Protocol.* New York: Shapolsky, 1991.

Davis, Stanley, Ph.D. *Future Perfect.* Reading, MA: Addison-Wesley, 1987.

De Tocqueville, Alexis. *Democracy in America.* New York: Doubleday, 1969.

Ehrlich, Paul, Ph.D. *The Population Bomb.* New York: Ballantine, 1968.

Felleman, Hazel, editor. *The Best Loved Poems.* Garden City, NY: Doubleday, 1936.

Fritz, Robert. *The Path of Least Resistance: Learning to Become the Creative Force in Your Own Life.* New York: Fawcett Columbine, 1989.

Galbraith, John Kenneth. *The Nature of Mass Poverty.* Cambridge, MA: Harvard University Press, 1979.

Gilder, George. *Microcosm.* New York: Simon & Schuster, 1989.

Harris, Louis. *Inside America.* New York: Vintage, 1987.

Hemphill, Barbara. *Taming the Paper Tiger.* Washington, DC: Hemphill & Associates, 1989.

Huxley, Aldous. *Brave New World.* New York: Harper & Row, 1946.

McLuhan, Marshall, Ph.D., and Quentin Fiore. *The Medium Is the Message.* New York: Bantam, 1966.

Postman, Neil, Ph.D. *Amusing Ourselves to Death: Public Discourse in the Age of Television*. New York: Viking, 1985.

Rifkin, Jeremy. *Time Wars: The Primary Conflict in Human History*. New York: Henry Holt, 1987.

Rose, Kenneth. *The Organic Clock*. New York: Wiley, 1988.

Schickel, Richard. *Intimate Strangers: The Culture of Celebrity*. New York: Doubleday, 1987.

Smith, Richard, and Linda Moore. *The Average Book*. New York: Rutledge Press, 1981.

Sugarman, Joseph. *Success Forces*. Chicago: Contemporary Books, 1980.

Taffel, Dr. Ron. *Parenting by Heart: How to Connect with Your Kids in the Face of Too Much Advice, Too Many Pressures, and Never Enough Time*. Reading, MA: Addison-Wesley, 1991.

Toffler, Alvin. *Future Shock*. New York: Random House, 1970.

Toffler, Alvin. *The Third Wave*. New York: Morrow, 1980.

Veblen, Thorstein. *The Theory of the Leisure Class*. New York: Modern Library, 1934.

Watts, Alan. *The Wisdom of Insecurity*. New York: Random House, 1968.

ABOUT THE AUTHOR

Jeff Davidson has developed a worldwide reputation for producing action-oriented books that offer complete systems to readers for accomplishing their goals.

His previous seventeen books, focusing on career enhancement, entrepreneurism, and personal achievement, have brought him considerable acclaim. At the age of forty, however, he established new career and life priorities to which he now directs his attention.

Breathing Space: Living and Working at a Comfortable Pace in a Sped-Up Society is the culmination of Jeff's eleven-year quest to determine why we have become a time-pressed culture, and, individually and collectively, what we can do about it. This focus area has rapidly become Jeff's most requested speaking topic.

A professional speaker and certified management consultant, Jeff is frequently asked to speak to groups across the country. He has appeared on *CBS Nightwatch, Ask Washington, It's Your Money* (FNN), *Nation's Business Today, America in the Morning, AP Radio, United Stations Radio Network,* and *CNCN* Canada. He has had 2,150 articles published since 1982 in hundreds of magazines, including *Working Woman, Marketing News, Boardroom Reports, Management Quarterly, Entrepreneur, Female Executive, Creative Age, Tomorrow's Business Leader, Business and Society Review,* and *Collegiate Woman,* among hundreds of others. In 1991, Jeff's articles reached 12.5 million readers.

Jeff has also been the repeat subject of feature articles in the *Washington Post, Miami Herald, Los Angeles Times, Christian Science Monitor, Chicago Tribune, Denver Times,* and dozens of other periodicals.

FROM THE AUTHOR

Send me your choices related to *Breathing Spaces.*

Yes. Send me a self-addressed stamped envelope with your eight to ten key choices. In exactly twelve months I'll return your list to you.

Chances are you make grand lists but then don't look at them. By getting your choices list back in twelve months, you can see how far you've moved!

Send your choices list to:

Choices
Jeff Davidson, MBA, CMC
3713 S. George Mason Drive #705W
Falls Church, VA 22041-3733

Additional copies of *Breathing Space* may be ordered by sending a check for $10.95 (please add the following for postage and handling: $2.00 for the first copy, $1.00 for each added copy) to:

MasterMedia Limited
16 East 72nd Street
New York, NY 10021
(212) 260-5600
(800) 334-8232

Jeff Davidson is available for speeches, conventions, annual meetings, or retreats. Please contact MasterMedia's Speakers' Bureau for availability and fee arrangements. Call Tony Colao at (908) 359-1612; fax: (908) 359-1647.

Other MasterMedia Books

THE PREGNANCY AND MOTHERHOOD DIARY: Planning the First Year of Your Second Career, by Susan Schiffer Stautberg, is the first and only undated appointment diary that shows how to manage pregnancy and career. ($12.95 spiralbound)

CITIES OF OPPORTUNITY: Finding the Best Place to Work, Live and Prosper in the 1990's and Beyond, by Dr. John Tepper Marlin, explores the job and living options for the next decade and into the next century. This consumer guide and handbook, written by one of the world's experts on cities, selects and features forty-six American cities and metropolitan areas. ($13.95 paper, $24.95 cloth)

THE DOLLARS AND SENSE OF DIVORCE, The Financial Guide for Women, by Judith Briles, is the first book to combine practical tips on overcoming the legal hurdles with planning before, during and after divorce ($10.95 paper)

OUT THE ORGANIZATION: How Fast Could You Find a New Job?, by Madeleine and Robert Swain, is written for the millions of Americans whose jobs are no longer safe, whose companies are not loyal and who face futures of uncertainty. It gives advice on finding a new job or starting your own business. ($11.95 paper, $17.95 cloth)

AGING PARENTS AND YOU: A Complete Handbook to Help You Help Your Elders Maintain a Healthy, Productive and Independent Life, by Eugenia Anderson-Ellis and Marsha Dryan, is a complete guide to providing care to aging relatives. It gives practical advice and resources to the adults who are helping their elders lead productive and independent lives. ($9.95 paper)

CRITICISM IN YOUR LIFE: How to Give It, How to Take It, How to Make It Work for You, by Dr. Deborah Bright, offers practical advice, in an upbeat, readable and realistic fashion, for turning criticism into control. Charts and diagrams guide the reader into managing criticism from bosses, spouses, children, friends, neighbors and in-laws. ($9.95 paper, $17.95 cloth)

BEYOND SUCCESS: How Volunteer Service Can Help You Begin Making a Life Instead of Just a Living, by John F. Raynolds III and Eleanor Raynolds, C.B.E., is a unique how-to book targeted to business and professional people considering volunteer work, senior citizens who wish to fill leisure time meaningfully and students trying out various career options. The book is filled with interviews with celebrities, CEOs and average citizens who talk about the benefits of service work. ($9.95 paper, $19.95 cloth)

MANAGING IT ALL: Time-Saving Ideas for Career, Family, Relationships and Self, by Beverly Benz Treuille and Susan Schiffer Stautberg, is written for women who are juggling careers and families. Over two hundred career women (ranging from a TV anchorwoman to an investment banker) were interviewed. The book contains many humorous anecdotes on saving time and improving the quality of life for self and family. ($9.95 paper)

REAL LIFE 101: (Almost) Surviving Your First Year Out of College, by Susan Kleinman, supplies welcome advice to those facing "real life" for the first time, focusing on work, money, health and how to deal with freedom and responsibility. ($9.95 paper)

YOUR HEALTHY BODY, YOUR HEALTHY LIFE: How to Take Control of Your Medical Destiny, by Donald B. Louria, M.A., provides precise advice and strategies that will help you to live a long and healthy life. Learn also about nutrition, exercise, vitamins and medication, as well as how to control risk factors for major diseases. ($12.95 paper)

THE CONFIDENCE FACTOR: How Self-Esteem Can Change Your Life, by Judith Briles, is based on a nationwide survey of six thousand men and women. Briles explores why women so often feel a lack of self-confidence and have a poor opinion of themselves. She offers step-by-step advice on becoming the person you want to be. ($18.95 cloth)

THE SOLUTION TO POLLUTION: 101 Things You Can Do to Clean Up Your Environment, by Laurence Sombke, offers step-by-step techniques on how to conserve more energy, start a recycling center, choose biodegradable products and proceed with individual environmental cleanup projects. ($7.95 paper)

TAKING CONTROL OF YOUR LIFE: The Secrets of Successful Enterprising Women, by Gail Blanke and Kathleen Walas, is based on the authors' professional experience with Avon Products' Women of Enterprise Awards, given each year to outstanding women entrepreneurs. The authors offer a specific plan to help you gain control over your life and include business tips and quizzes as well as beauty and lifestyle information. ($17.95 cloth)

SIDE-BY-SIDE STRATEGIES: How Two-Career Couples Can Thrive in the Nineties, by Jane Hershey Cuozzo and S. Diane Graham, describes how two-career couples can learn the difference between competing with a spouse and becoming a supportive power partner. ($10.95 paper)

DARE TO CONFRONT! How to Intervene When Someone You Care About Has an Alcohol or Drug Problem, by Bob Wright and Deborah George Wright, shows the reader how to use the step-by-step methods of professional interventionists to motivate drug-dependent people to accept the help they need. ($17.95 cloth)

WORK WITH ME! How to Make the Most of Office Support Staff, by Betsy Lazary, shows how to find, train, and nurture the "perfect" assistant and how best to utilize your support staff professionals. ($9.95 paper)

MANN FOR ALL SEASONS: Wit and Wisdom from The Washington Post's *Judy Mann,* by Judy Mann, shows the columnist at her best as she writes about women, families and the politics of the women's revolution. ($9.95 paper, $19.95 cloth)

THE SOLUTION TO POLLUTION IN THE WORKPLACE, by Laurence Sombke, Terry M. Robertson and Elliot M. Kaplan, supplies employees with everything they need to know about cleaning up their workspace, including recycling, using energy efficiently, conserving water and buying recycled products and nontoxic supplies. ($9.95 paper)

THE ENVIRONMENTAL GARDENER: The Solution to Pollution for Lawns and Gardens, by Laurence Sombke, focuses on what each of us can do to protect our endangered plant life. A practical sourcebook and shopping guide. ($8.95 paper)

THE LOYALTY FACTOR: Building Trust in Today's Workplace, by Carol Kinsey Goman, Ph.D., offers techniques for restoring commitment and loyalty in the workplace. ($9.95 paper)

DARE TO CHANGE YOUR JOB—AND YOUR LIFE, by Carole Kanchier, Ph.D., provides a look at career growth and development throughout the life cycle. ($10.95 paper)

MISS AMERICA: In Pursuit of the Crown, by Ann-Marie Bivans, is an authorized guidebook to the Pageant, containing eyewitness accounts, complete historical data, and a realistic look at the trials and triumphs of potential Miss Americas. ($27.50 cloth)

SUMMARY OF

BREATHING SPACE

The Reality of Life in the Over-information Era:

❏ The world of less than 5.3 billion people is gone and is never coming back.
❏ More information is generated in a day than you could comfortably ingest in the rest of your life.
❏ There is no keeping up: there are only choices to make about where you want to devote your attention.
❏ You can't afford to pay attention to everyone else's fifteen minutes of fame.

Principles:

❏ Choose a few priorities and a handful of goals to support each of those priorities.
❏ Employ Operation Clean Sweep, daily, if necessary.
❏ Condition your environments.
❏ Manage the beforehand.
❏ Use multiple stations.
❏ Actively limit intake overglut and packratism.
❏ Constantly seek completions.
❏ Live in the moment.
❏ Keep choosing what you want.
❏ Help others attain Breathing Space.

Reflections:

❏ You are whole and complete right now.
❏ Our society does not have to accommodate the over-glut, if individually each of us chooses to diminish it.

Everyone Needs Breathing Space; Everyone Can Choose to Have It.